THE IRISH MAJORS

Irish Golf's Magnificent Seven

THE IRISH MAJORS

Irish Golf's Magnificent Seven

PHILIP REID ∿

Gill & Macmillan

Gill & Macmillan
Hume Avenue, Park West, Dublin 12
with associated companies throughout the world
www.gillmacmillanbooks.ie

© Philip Reid 2012
978 07171 5374 9

Index compiled by Kate Murphy
Typography design by Make Communication
Print origination by Carole Lynch
Printed by ScandBook AB, Sweden

This book is typeset in Linotype Minion and
Neue Helvetica.

The paper used in this book comes from the wood
pulp of managed forests. For every tree felled, at least
one tree is planted, thereby renewing natural
resources.

A CIP catalogue record for this book is available from
the British Library.

5 4 3 2 1

CONTENTS

INTRODUCTION

I remember the very first time I saw Nick Faldo in the flesh. It was at the Irish Open at Portmarnock Golf Club in 1986. I don't know why but the tall and somewhat gangly — at the time — Englishman always held a peculiar fascination for me: perhaps it was his dedication to the game, or how he always seemed to be in the right, even if others held seemingly strong arguments.

On that day in June, Faldo had not yet gained the status of being a Major champion. If anything, he was enduring the anguish of a swing change that had many observers, especially those in the media centre, wondering if he had lost his senses. After all, in the early part of the 1980s, Faldo had won numerous times on the PGA European Tour and topped the Order of Merit, the money list, in 1983. He had even won one of those ghastly tartan jackets for his win in the Heritage Classic on the US Tour.

But, deep down, Faldo knew he needed to reconstruct his swing if he was to attain the 'Holy Grail' which, for any professional golfer worth his salt, is a Major championship.

So it was that I followed Faldo for a number of holes, simply to see what he had become. To be honest, it didn't look like much. He shot a round of 81 on that wonderful seaside course and missed the cut. Faldo, though, was to be ultimately proven right: the following year he won his first of six Majors.

The 1987 British Open at Muirfield in Scotland where he parred all 18 holes of the final round for a one-stroke winning margin over American Paul Azinger proved to be Faldo's breakthrough Major and, thereafter, there was no stopping him. He became the greatest European player, in terms of Major wins, which is the standard used by every professional, of modern times. In all, he won three Open championships and three Masters titles.

Ironically, that Irish Open of 1986 was won by none other than Seve Ballesteros. Although he didn't win as many Major titles as Faldo, the charismatic and passionate Spaniard — in many ways the opposite to the Englishman — personified all that was great about European golf. His play was swashbuckling, without fear. Seve was a golfing matador. And the people everywhere loved him.

Ballesteros won his first Major in 1979 as a 22-year old in the Open championship at Royal Lytham & St Annes. He won five Majors, one less than Faldo. The whiplash swing of Ballesteros was something to behold, even if it caught up with him later in his career when constantly troubled by a bad back. Sadly, Ballesteros left this life too early. In May of 2011, he died from brain cancer. He was 54.

As the South African Ernie Els put it of Ballesteros's appeal, 'Seve was Tiger before Tiger was Tiger.' Many of the tributes to Ballesteros used words such as 'genius' and 'legend' and, for sure, he was all those and more. He had the ability to imagine shots that nobody else dared hit, like the three-wood he took from a cavernous bunker to the edge of the final green at the PGA National in Florida during the 1983 Ryder Cup.

The Majors gave him a special stage, as they should. Ballesteros won three British Opens and two US Masters, with arguably his most precious title coming at the home of golf in the 1984 British Open at St Andrews. On that day, what was to become an iconic image — of Seve fist-pumping the air on the 18th green — was born.

Anyone who came in contact with Seve couldn't help but be pulled in by his magnetism, for he had a charisma where even his occasional scowl came across as gracious.

My own special Seve moment dates back to the Irish Open at Fota Island in Co. Cork in 2002. The call to play on Seve's team in the pre-tournament pro-am had come on the Monday — which necessitated a roadside stop in the Co. Laois village of Mountrath in order to digest the news — and the build-up to sharing the same tee boxes and fairways and greens as the legend brought trepidation to mix with the anticipation.

On that Wednesday, the alarm call came at seven o'clock. But I'd already been awake for two full hours, the nervous tension playing tricks with body and mind. On the first tee, along with the other amateurs Con Horgan and Frank Murray, there was no sense of aloofness from the great man. He was one of us, human. Smiling. Normal.

And, yet, throughout the round, his impulse to solve imperfection was incessant. After a wayward drive, he stood on the tee box — his arms raised above his shoulders — as he sought the perfect takeaway. Not only that, but there was a compulsion to fix imperfections in others. 'Me! Demasiado rapido . . . too fast, Philip . . . Move your head,' he would say. 'More. Okay, hit.'

Ballesteros was a man who loved to be in control, and when his swing went, he wasn't. 'When I was playing good,' he was to remark, 'I knew I was in control. I was in control of the galleries, of the golf courses, even the other players. I knew I would win and winning was enough.'

The Majors gave Ballesteros the opportunity to show his greatness to the world. And that is what the Majors are about. They ask the toughest questions on the toughest courses with the toughest fields and, more often than not, the best man will emerge the winner.

There is something about the Majors, championships which define the careers of so many. And the remarkable thing about recent years is that Irish players — excluded from the fold for so long — have gatecrashed this elite club.

Did any of us truly see this coming? Not in our wildest dreams, if we are to be honest.

Did we believe the teenager who turned up with blond highlighted streaks in his hair at the Mullingar Scratch Cup in his youth would claim a Claret Jug? Darren Clarke did.

Did we think the Dubliner who once aspired to follow his father into the world of Gaelic football, only to realise it was a futile dream when left sitting on the Croke Park turf once too often by a young fella called Dessie Farrell in a schools match, would become a multi-Major champion? Pádraig Harrington did.

Did we see the day when Graeme McDowell would raise the US Open trophy high above his head as the waves splashed on the rocks by the 18th green at Pebble Beach Links on the Monterey Peninsula? G-Mac believed.

Did we envision Rory McIlroy recovering from his Masters travails to break record after record in getting his name engraved below McDowell's on the US Open Trophy? Honestly . . ?

This golden generation of Irish golf has delivered riches

beyond belief. Where once it seemed an impossible dream to attempt to follow in the footsteps of Fred Daly — the 1947 Open champion — as a Major winner, the deeds of Harrington, McDowell, McIlroy and Clarke have allowed us to cherish the moment. And to believe that there are more to come.

Why should it end now?

Chapter 1 ∿

THE ALLURE OF THE MAJORS

Golf is a multibillion euro industry, with courses all over the globe and seemingly a tournament played somewhere every week of the year. But each year there are four championships which stand out and which are the most coveted of them all: they are the Majors, three of which are played in the United States — the Masters tournament, the US Open and the US PGA — and one of them, the oldest of them all, the Open championship, which is played on a rota of links courses in Scotland and England.

The allure of the Majors is an overwhelming one, for players and golf fans alike. As in any sport, it is the history of championships — great winners on great courses — that has expanded these tournaments into the most supreme of tests and which has made them a prize greater than any other in the sport.

Where and how did it all start? As with most things, those who organised the very first Open in 1860 could scarcely have imagined how it would evolve into one of sport's greatest events. The inaugural championship was played at Prestwick Golf Club: there was no prize money, but the winner received the Challenge Belt for a year. Clubs from around England and Scotland were invited to send not more than three professional players to compete in the three-round competition played on the 12-hole links course.

Only eight players, all from Scotland, played in the first British Open which took place in windy conditions and in front of a small gallery. Willie Park became the first champion — and became the custodian of the red Moroccan belt with a silver buckle and embellished with emblems — after he fired rounds of 55-59-60 for a 36-hole aggregate of 174, two strokes better than the pre-championship favourite Tom Morris.

Golf's Majors were up and running: not that they knew it at the time, for the term 'Major' only came to be associated with the biggest tournaments many years later. Indeed, the original four Majors were the (British) Open, the British Amateur, the US Open and the US Amateur championships.

Only one man, Bobby Jones — Robert Tyre Jones Jnr — has had the distinction of winning the so-called 'Grand Slam' of all four Majors in the same year, a feat he achieved in 1930 when he won the British Amateur, the British Open, the US Open and the US Amateur. He retired two months after that monumental feat and, ironically, his creation of Augusta National Golf Club in the following years, where he hosted the Masters tournament, was the catalyst for the evolution of the modern four Majors as the two amateur championships were dropped in favour of the addition of the Masters and the US PGA.

Nowadays, and retrospectively, the four professional Majors — the (British) Open, the Masters, the US Open and the US PGA — have become the greatest prizes in the sport. And, naturally enough, given the course set-up and the quality of the fields, they are also the hardest won of all tournaments.

The early days of the Open saw it dominated by Scots, who won the first 29 championships. The original prize, that of the Challenge Belt, was replaced by the famed Claret Jug in 1872 after Young Tom Morris won a third successive championship in 1870 and was allowed to keep the belt.

After Young Tom's hat-trick of wins, there was no championship staged — for lack of a prize — in 1871. It proved to be a short hiatus, and moves to revive the competition resumed the following year. The minutes of the Royal and Ancient Golf Club (based at St Andrews in Scotland) stated that the green committee had been 'empowered to enter into communication with other clubs with a view to effecting a revival of the Championship Belt, and they were authorised to contribute a sum not exceeding £15 from the funds of the club'.

Later in 1872, agreement was reached between the three clubs — Prestwick, the Honourable Company of Edinburgh Golfers (Muirfield) and the Royal and Ancient Golf Club — that the winner would receive a medal and that a new trophy, rather than a belt, would be commissioned. The trophy, however, wasn't ready in time to be presented to that year's champion, Young Tom Morris, who won the championship for a fourth — and final — time. He would have won more but for his tragic death at the age of 24.

Since 1873, when Tom Kidd triumphed, the Claret Jug has been presented to the Champion Golfer of the Year.

The Open is run by the R&A and played annually on a rota of courses in Scotland and England. The only occasion the event was played outside of those two countries was in 1951, when Max Faulkner claimed the Claret Jug at Royal Portrush Golf Club in

Northern Ireland. Four years earlier, at Hoylake in 1947, Fred Daly had become the first Irishman to win a Major when he claimed the Claret Jug. The wait for the next Irishman to follow in Daly's footsteps would last for a full 60 years, until Pádraig Harrington triumphed in the Open at Carnoustie in 2007.

——

Which of the four Majors is the most coveted? There can be no definitive weighted measurement. Many will say that the Open, as the oldest and the most open of them all in that international qualifying occurs in places like Australia, South Africa and Asia, is the pre-eminent championship; others, mainly Americans, will claim the US Open, run by the USGA and which traditionally has the toughest course set-up, deserves such an honour; and, despite its limited invitation-only field, there are those who believe the Masters, the only Major to return each year to the same course and run by Augusta National Golf Club, is the one which captures most the imagination of player and public alike.

The fourth Major — the US PGA, run by the PGA of America — has always seemed to live in the shadows somewhat of the other three championships. Although it has a history which dates back to 1916, it was for a long time perceived as the one with the weakest field and often played on courses barely adequate for such a Major championship.

In recent years, however, such arguments seem dated: the courses now used for the US PGA are as good as any used for the US Open and changes implemented in recent years have seen the strength of the field improve to the point where the US PGA is inclined to have more of the world's top-100 ranked players participating than any other of the Majors.

Down through the years, the Majors have produced many wonderful champions. Of all the golf tournaments throughout the year, and there are many, the Majors are the most prized of all and consequently the hardest of all to win. There have been many great Major victories, and many tales of heartache.

There is no disputing who has been the greatest champion of them all, however. Jack Nicklaus was born in Columbus, Ohio, and holds the record number of professional Majors won: when he captured his last, the 1986 Masters, it brought his total to 18 victories. If there were those who felt it was only a matter of time before Tiger Woods — who had pictures of Nicklaus posted on his bedroom wall as a child — broke the Golden Bear's record, injuries as well as the fall-out caused by his much-publicised extra-marital affairs have combined to make that less of the formality it once seemed.

Before Nicklaus there was Walter Hagen. A product of the so-called Roaring Twenties, Hagen got his first introduction to the sport working as a caddie at Rochester Country Club in New York where he started to play using clubs borrowed from the members. He created his own four-hole course in a cow pasture. He left school before his teenage years and worked in a variety of jobs, from car repairer to apprentice mandolin maker, until given a route into his true vocation: as a golf club professional.

Hagen had a reputation for his natty fashion sense and his capacity to party through the night, but nobody worked harder preparing for tournaments, and he carried with him an assurance and self-belief on to the course that opponents simply couldn't match. He won nine Majors — two US Opens, five US PGAS, including four in a row from 1924, and four British Opens — but his best years had passed by the time the Masters was created. He only played a handful of times at Augusta National, with a best finish of tied-11th in the 1936 tournament.

Nicklaus's record of 18 Major wins would appear set to remain intact for the foreseeable future. The American won his first Major — the US Open — in 1962 and amassed his array of titles through the 60s, 70s and 80s before he conceded that the old bones couldn't compete to the level required any longer. When his work was done, Nicklaus had claimed four US Opens (1962, 67, 72 and 80), six US Masters titles (63, 65, 66, 72, 75 and 86), five US PGAS (63, 71, 73, 75 and 80) and three British Opens (66, 70 and 78).

As remarkable as Nicklaus's haul of 18 Major titles is, he also finished runner-up on 19 occasions. The legendary Bobby Jones once remarked of Nicklaus: 'He plays a game with which I am not familiar.' Through the years, Jones was not alone in wondering how golf's greatest Major champion continually found a way to get the job done. Nicklaus lived his life atop leaderboards and remained hugely competitive for over three decades.

Of all his Major wins, the 1986 Masters — his 18th — was the most poignant. To win his first Major at the 1962 US Open, Nicklaus had defeated his long-time rival Arnold Palmer in a play-off. His record sixth Masters success came at the age of 46 when it seemed he had already achieved all there was to achieve in the sport.

In that 1986 Masters, Nicklaus had gone into the final round in tied-ninth position and four shots adrift of 54-hole leader Greg Norman. Between the 'Golden Bear' and the 'Great White

Shark' were some of the finest players in the game: Seve Ballesteros, Bernhard Langer, Tom Watson. In truth, it seemed Nicklaus's cause as he set out on that final round was a lost one. But he shot a closing round 65 — which featured a homeward run of just 30 strokes on the back nine — as he compiled a 72-hole aggregate of 279, nine-under-par. It gave him a one-shot victory margin over Norman and Tom Kite.

Nicklaus was also involved in one of the great British Open final rounds in that Major's long and rich history. Only in 1977 he came out on the wrong side of a fascinating contest with Watson: in what became known as the 'Duel in the Sun', the championship at Turnberry in Scotland saw the two Americans battle to the wire before Watson added the Claret Jug to the Green Jacket he had won at Augusta earlier in the year.

'This is what it's all about, isn't it?' Watson had asked Nicklaus on the 16th tee of the final round as they were tied at 11-under-par for the championship, 10 strokes ahead of eventual third-placed finisher Hubert Green. 'You bet it is,' replied Nicklaus. Watson had just sunk a 60 footer for birdie from off the green on the 15th to move level with the man 10 years his senior.

As it transpired, the difference between the two men came on the par 5 17th hole. Watson birdied and Nicklaus, incredibly, missed his own birdie putt from three feet. That Nicklaus conjured up a closing birdie on the 18th, despite his swing being affected by a nearby gorse bush on his approach shot, didn't matter. So too did Watson manage a birdie. Watson shot a final round 65, for 268, to Nicklaus's 66 for a one-shot win.

The importance of the Majors to Nicklaus can be gauged from the recollections of his very first appearance in one. Nicklaus made a sentimental appearance in the 2000 US Open at Pebble Beach, where he missed the cut. Yet he could recall his first appearance in the 1957 US Open — as a 17-year old at Inverness, where Dick Mayer triumphed in a play-off over Cary Middlecoff — and what shots he had played over the opening holes.

'I hit a three-wood off the first tee down the middle of the fairway, hit a seven-iron on the green about 35 feet and I made the putt. Parred the second hole. I parred the third hole, and my name went up on the leaderboard. I drove it in the left rough at number four, didn't hit it on the green in three, made double-bogey. My name went off the leaderboard and that was about what I remember.'

One other thing which Nicklaus remembered of that first appearance in the US Open was watching the legendary Ben Hogan in practice in the days before the tournament. Sadly, Hogan never got to start that championship, as his back — a product of the car accident that very nearly finished his career — spasmed on the driving range before his scheduled tee time.

Hogan — from Dublin, Texas — won nine Majors in his career: four US Opens, two US Masters, two US PGAS and one British Open. He overcame many things to achieve greatness, not least the appalling injuries sustained in a head-on collision with a Greyhound bus.

A late bloomer, Hogan's initial years on tour from 1931 to 39 — where he battled a propensity to hook his ball off the tee, which only served to make him stay on the practice range longer than anyone else — brought stories of a poverty-stricken golfer who jumped fences to claim oranges from orchards so that he could eat. His first individual tour win came in 1940 and he topped the US money list for three successive years up to 1943 before he joined the US military for the final two years of the Second World War.

Hogan returned from the conflict with more intensity than ever, and he captured his first Major win in the 1946 US PGA at Portland in Oregon. At the time, the US PGA was played in a match play format and Hogan out-duelled Ed Oliver to win by a 6 & 4 margin in the final.

Fate intervened in February 1949, when a 10-ton bus swerved into his car on a foggy morning. Hogan — who had added the 1948 US Open and the 1948 US PGA to his curriculum vitae of Majors — threw himself across the passenger seat to protect his wife Valerie, and quite possibly avoided death by doing so. But he sustained serious injuries: a double-fracture of the pelvis, a fractured collar-bone, a left ankle fracture, a chipped rib and blood clots in his lungs. There was a doubt Hogan would ever walk again, never mind play golf.

Hogan, though, resumed his golfing activities towards the end of the year and returned to the US Tour for the 1950 season. Later that same year, he won a second US Open title — at Merion — and the man known as the 'Hawk' continued to rebuild his strength and to work incessantly on the practice range in his quest for further Majors, which had become his obsession. He barely played in regular tournaments, reserving all his focus for the ones that mattered most.

In the 1953 season, Hogan produced arguably the greatest series of performances in the Majors of all time: in the Masters at Augusta National he played what he called the best golf of his life. He shot a then-record aggregate of 274 and finished five strokes clear of Porky Oliver to claim a second Green Jacket, awarded to the winner of the Masters each year.

Hogan followed up his win in the Masters by winning the US Open at Oakmont, where he finished 3-3-3 over one of the toughest finishing stretches in the championship and claimed a six-stroke winning margin over Sam Snead.

Time and time again Hogan was reminded that his CV was incomplete unless he managed to win a British Open. In the summer of 1953, he went about the task of adding the Claret Jug to his collection. That year's championship was played at Carnoustie and Hogan arrived in advance to map out how he would conquer the links. He did, and won by four strokes from a quartet of futile pursuers.

Hogan had won the first three Majors of the year, and had given himself an opportunity to do what no man had ever done — or managed since — which was to win all four Majors in the one season. A Grand Slam. But Hogan felt that the demands of the US PGA, still in match play format, would be too great on his body and didn't play the final Major of the season. He never played in a British Open again, and he never won another Major after that miracle year of 53. But his reputation as arguably the purest striker of a ball in the game's history has lived on through the years.

If Hogan earned a reputation as the game's purest striker, Arnold Palmer — a winner of seven Major titles — was the player who revolutionised the sport in terms of global popularity. His arrival on the scene came at a time when the televising of golf was in its infancy. Together, Palmer and TV worked their magic.

Palmer's favourite tournament of all was the Masters, where he became the first player to win four Green Jackets. He won at

Augusta National for the first time in 1958 — when he had one stroke to spare over Fred Hawkins and Doug Ford — and added further Masters' titles in even sequence in 60, 62 and 64. His other Major wins came in the US Open (60) and British Open (61 and 62) and there was always a sense that there would have been more if not for the fact that much of his career overlapped with the younger Nicklaus. The real shame, though, is that Palmer never managed to win a career Grand Slam. The US PGA, despite three runner-up finishes, eluded him throughout his career.

But then golfers have always had to contend with rivalry. It has been a feature through the years from the sport's earliest days. In the 1890s and into the 1910s we had the original trendsetters: Harry Vardon, J. H. Taylor and James Braid, a group of golfers known as the 'Triumvirate'; in the 1920s and into the 30s you had Walter Hagen, Gene Sarazen and amateur Bobby Jones; in the 40s, Byron Nelson, Sam Snead and Ben Hogan. Later, Nicklaus and Palmer, and Gary Player and Tom Watson.

Only five players in the history of the sport have managed to win career Grand Slams. Two of them, Nicklaus and Tiger Woods, have done so multiple times. The other three — Hogan, Sarazen and Player — achieved the feat once. Of the quintet, the only non-American is Player, a South African who defied his slight stature with a giant personality and a work ethic that was at odds with many players who took delight in claiming they had never seen the inside of a gym.

Player won nine Majors in the era of Nicklaus and Palmer, which truthfully says all there needs to be said about his status in the game. Indeed, that Augusta National invited him to join Nicklaus and Palmer as ceremonial starters at the 2012 Masters was an acknowledgment of that. He was back as part of the so-called 'Big Three', a marketing tool used by Mark McCormack's International Management Group to promote his men.

The diversity of Player's wins was certainly impressive: he won his first of three British Opens in the 1959 championship at Muirfield, where he came from eight shots back at the midway stage to win. He won three Masters, two US PGAS and one US Open. All together the haul of nine Majors entitled him to a place alongside Nicklaus and Palmer, one of the 'Big Three'.

On and on it went — rivalries that fed the soul of the sport, which added to the allure of the Majors.

In the 70s and into the 80s, however, a new dimension was added: after years of dominance by the Americans, European players re-emerged from the shadows. One man more than any other was responsible for the resurgence: Seve Ballesteros, who swashbuckled his way on to the Major scene when, at the age of 22, the Spaniard captured the British Open title at Royal Lytham & St Annes on the west coast of England.

Ballesteros won five Majors in his career — three British Opens (79, 84 and 88) and two US Masters (80 and 83) — and he was the one who hit seemingly impossible golf shots, one after the other. He had good looks and charisma, and he played with a passion and emotion that nobody could emulate. Or sought to.

Two of his British Open wins came at Lytham. The first, in 1979, signalled the arrival of a new prince: he finished with a 72-hole total of 283, three shots in front of the great Nicklaus and his fellow-American Ben Crenshaw. Nine years later, in 1988, Ballesteros claimed a third Claret Jug and his second at Lytham when he finished with a total of 273, two shots clear of Zimbabwe's Nick Price.

That final round was one of the great finishes in championship golf and epitomised his magical qualities, as Ballesteros shot a closing 65. There was one breath-taking stretch of holes, from the sixth to the 13th, which Price covered in five-under and where he lost ground to his rival who negotiated the eight holes in six-under. Perhaps fate decreed that it should be Ballesteros's day: he wore the same trousers and the same sweater he had worn in the final round of 79!

Ballesteros was part of an exciting new generation of European golfers which included Sandy Lyle, Bernhard Langer, Ian Woosnam and Nick Faldo. A few years later, another Spaniard, José María Olazábal, joined the gang. All became Major winners, but it was Faldo who won more than any of them.

Faldo — who won three British Opens (87, 90 and 92) and three US Masters titles (89, 90 and 96) — has matured into one of the most polished of all the television commentators. In his heyday on the golf course the Englishman also demonstrated a single-minded dedication.

An example of Faldo's dedication to the cause — his own cause, naturally — was to reconstruct his swing under the tutelage of his then coach David Leadbetter in the mid-1980s. The upshot was a maiden Major win in the Open at Muirfield in 1987 when he reeled off 18 successive pars in the final round to defeat Paul Azinger and Rodger Davis by one shot. Faldo would win six Majors in 10 years, the last of them probably the most dramatic and memorable of them all.

That sixth Major title for Faldo came in the 1996 US Masters, a championship where Australian Greg Norman seemed set to finally deliver on his undoubted talents and claim a Green Jacket. It was the prize Norman wanted more than any other and the Great White Shark carried a six-shot lead over Faldo into the final round. The unthinkable happened, though. Norman lost, after he shot a final round 78 to Faldo's 67.

The following year, in 1997, the golfing world was pitched into a new dimension: Tiger Woods strode into Augusta National, the setting for Norman's meltdown the previous year, and announced his arrival as the greatest player of his generation and a man determined to overtake Nicklaus's record of 18 Major victories.

In that Masters of 97, Woods demonstrated his human frailties when he covered the opening nine holes in 40 strokes. Thereafter, golf's next superstar was as close to perfect as it was possible to be on a golf course; and, after Woods took a three-stroke lead at the halfway stage, it prompted none other than Nicklaus to para-phrase the words which Bobby Jones had used of him years earlier. 'It's a shame Bob Jones isn't here. He could have saved the words for me in 1963 for this young man, because he's playing a game we're certainly not familiar with.'

Woods had been a childhood phenomenon who made a seamless move into the professional ranks after an amateur career that saw him win three successive US Amateur Open titles. His performance in the 1997 Masters — where he won by 12 strokes — gave him a first Major championship title at the age of 21, and his status soared as he set out his stall to chase down Nicklaus's record.

In 2000, Woods failed to win the Masters. He only finished fifth. But he was to prove invincible in the other three Majors that season as he won the US Open by a record 15 strokes at Pebble Beach, the British Open by eight shots over the Old Course at St Andrews and took the US PGA — where he beat Bob May in a play-off — to confirm his superiority.

When Woods drove down Magnolia Lane into Augusta National Golf Club in April of 2001, he was poised to claim a fourth successive Major. It didn't constitute a 'Grand Slam' — winning all four Majors in the same season — but he went about claiming what became known as the 'Tiger Slam' with a comprehensive two-stroke win over runner-up David Duval. 'I've got all four trophies sitting on my coffee table,' said Woods as he basked in the knowledge that he was the greatest living golfer on the planet.

Woods's pursuit of Nicklaus stalled after he won a 14th Major title in the 2008 US Open at Torrey Pines, where he defeated Rocco Mediate in an 18-hole play-off. The trophy had barely been raised above his head when plans were made for Woods to undergo another operation on his troublesome knee. Then, his involvement in a car crash in November 2009 led to the revelations of numerous extra-marital affairs which ultimately led to divorce and a search for a new golf swing.

The perfect life didn't seem so perfect any longer, and that chase after Nicklaus became tougher than it ever was.

The manner in which Woods, in his prime, ticked off one box after another in his relentless and ruthless quest for Majors was at some odds with the experiences of his greatest rival Phil Mickelson. Time and time again, Mickelson came up short in his attempts to claim one of golf's greatest prizes.

Before he finally made the breakthrough and won his maiden Major at the 2004 Masters, Mickelson had knocked on the door so often in different Majors without ever being allowed in: he had finished third on no fewer than four occasions at the Masters; he had been twice runner-up in the US Open, and once runner-up in the US PGA.

Then in 2004 he found a way to win a Green Jacket — when he beat South African Ernie Els by one shot — and with that he found a key to the door. Mickelson, who also claimed the US PGA in 2005, has since added two further US Masters titles to his collection, in 2006 and 2010, and quite rightfully assumed a place at the top table when it comes to acknowledging great golfing deeds.

Mickelson's 12-year quest for a first Major after he turned professional only served to underline how tough it is for any player to win a Major. At least Mickelson managed to find a way to do so; other great players have gone through their careers without ever tasting such success.

In recent times, Colin Montgomerie is the most obvious example of just how hard it is to win a Major. Montgomerie carried the European Tour on his broad shoulders for over a decade, during which time he won seven successive PGA European Tour order of merits. He carried Europe to victory in the Ryder Cup with an audacity never seen before in the biennial match that pitted Europe's best against America's finest. Time and time again he stood up and was counted, except when it came to the Majors!

Montgomerie unquestionably deserved to win a Major in his career. He was certainly good enough, and he had his chances. The Scot finished runner-up on five occasions in Major championships, and on two occasions — the 1994 US Open to Els at Congressional and the 1995 US PGA to Steve Elkington at Riviera — he lost out in a play-off.

Perhaps Montgomerie's best chance of all, though, came in the 2006 US Open at the magnificent Winged Foot Country Club in New York. On the 72nd hole, Montgomerie found himself in the middle of the fairway off the tee and an eight-iron in his hand. A par four would have won the famed trophy, but he proceeded to run up a double-bogey six. It just wasn't to be for Europe's finest player of the 90s into the Noughties.

Indeed, after the seemingly year-on-year wins enjoyed by the so-called 'Big Five' of European golf —Ballesteros, Faldo, Lyle, Woosnam and Langer — and the couple of Masters jackets claimed by Seve's protégé José María Olazábal, it seemed that much of European golf's best times came in the Ryder Cup rather than the Majors.

Paul Lawrie, a Scot, had won the British Open at Carnoustie in 1999, but there wasn't to be another European winner of a Major until 2007. No fewer than 31 Major championships had come and gone when Pádraig Harrington stepped up to the mark and ended a number of droughts: he became the first Irish golfer since Fred Daly, in 1947, to win a Major; and he became the first European player since Lawrie, in 1999, to win a Major.

Nobody, though, could have anticipated that Harrington's first British Open triumph at Carnoustie would open the floodgates in the way it did.

———

The Majors, more than any other golf tournaments, have become the perfect stage for perfect golf shots.

SIX OF THE BEST

1935 US Masters
Augusta National Golf Club
GENE SARAZEN

It became known as 'the shot heard round the world'. In the final round of the 1935 US Masters, Gene Sarazen faced up to his approach shot on the par 5 15th hole. Many observers had already given the title to Craig Wood and saw Sarazen's pursuit down the final holes as being futile. Sarazen was paired with Walter Hagen for the final round. It was a convivial pairing. Hagen — out of contention — reminded Sarazen of the time he had jokingly arranged for a wheelchair to be brought out to him as he struggled home in the 1933 US Open.

On the 15th hole, Sarazen hit one of his best drives. He had put what he called a 'tail-end hook' on it and the ball ran on the firm fairways. But as he approached the ball, a huge roar erupted from the 18th green where Wood had rolled in a birdie putt to finish. As Sarazen — who was three behind — looked up the hill, he could make out the flashbulbs of the photographers as they captured Wood's image for the newspapers.

Sarazen figured he needed to finish eagle-par-birdie-birdie if he was to match Wood's total of 282. Having consulted with his caddie — called 'Stovepipe' — he decided to use a new club in his bag, a four-wood, for the 235-yard shot. The shot to the green, guarded by Rae's Creek, had a low trajectory and Sarazen chased after it so that he could see how close it would finish to the hole. He holed out for an albatross two, and went on to defeat Wood in the following day's play-off.

1979 British Open
Royal Lytham & St Annes
SEVE BALLESTEROS
In the final round, Seve Ballesteros stood on the 16th tee and elected to play a 3-wood rather than his driver. For safety. However, the Spanish maestro's tee shot was an errant one and curled its way into a temporary parking lot set up for television production vehicles. Fortunately for Ballesteros, the area was deemed to be in play by the rules officials.

Off a bone-hard surface, Ballesteros bounced a lofty sand wedge and sent the ball to nestle 15 feet from the hole. He rolled in the birdie putt *en route* to a maiden Major title. His deeds of escapology earned him the nickname, the 'Car Park Champion'.

1982 US Open
Pebble Beach Links
TOM WATSON
The par 3 17th hole at Pebble Beach had long had a reputation as a graveyard for golfing hopes. And when Tom Watson's two-iron tee shot in the final round of the US Open finished in heavy grass on the upslope beyond the green, it seemed that his quest for the title had gone.

'Get it close,' said Watson's caddie, Bruce Edwards.

'I'm not gonna get it close. I'm gonna make it,' replied the player. Which is exactly what Watson did, as he claimed a maiden US Open and his sixth Major with a chip-in from just over five yards that nobody other than the player himself believed was possible.

1986 US PGA
Inverness Golf Club, Ohio
BOB TWAY
Why Greg Norman became the fall guy in so many Majors is anyone's guess. It seemed to happen time and time again, and none was more heart-breaking than the manner of his loss to Bob Tway in the US PGA at Inverness.

Norman had a four-stroke lead with eight holes to play as the championship dragged into a Monday finish due to a rain delay, and the two protagonists arrived at the 18th hole tied for the lead. Norman seemed to have the upper hand after the two played their approach shots. The Australian's ball was on the edge of the green; Tway's found a greenside bunker. But Tway blasted his ball out of the sand trap . . . and into the hole for a winning birdie.

2005 US Masters
Augusta National Golf Club
TIGER WOODS
On the par 3 16th hole, Tiger Woods missed the green with his tee shot and walked up to his ball, only to find it had rolled up against the second cut of rough. He faced a very difficult chip shot of 25 yards up a slope to an audaciously fast green.

Woods's chip — aimed well left of the flag — barely made the putting surface but then started to move slowly but surely down towards the cup. The ball stopped, slowed down as it approached the hole, but then somehow found another couple of rolls and fell into the hole. The image gave Nike a ready-made marketing campaign and the birdie enabled Woods to get into a play-off with Chris DiMarco, which Woods won at the first hole.

2012 US Masters
Augusta National Golf Club
BUBBA WATSON

When Bubba Watson pulled his drive on the par 4 10th hole — the second hole of a sudden-death play-off with Louis Oosthuizen — it seemed that his dream of a maiden Major had disappeared with his ball into the pine straw amidst the towering trees that lined the right side of the fairway.

Watson couldn't see the green and only had a narrow escape gap between trees and bushes and overhanging branches. With 164 yards to the hole, the left-hander used a TV tower as his marker and dispatched the ball towards it. Keeping the initial flight low to avoid tree limbs, he audaciously hooked a 52° gap wedge some 40 yards. The ball came to rest 15 feet from the pin and he two-putted for victory.

———

7/2235751.

THE TROPHIES
The us Masters

The winner of the Masters receives a trophy — a replica of the Augusta National Golf Club clubhouse — which is made of more than 900 pieces of silver and rests on a pedestal around which are the silver bands bearing the winners' names. The trophy was introduced in 1961 and is permanently housed in the clubhouse. Since 1993, a sterling replica of the original has been presented to the Masters champion.

The winner of the Masters receives a number of other perks. Probably the most famous of all is the Green Jacket, which the champion is allowed to take with him for the first year before returning it to the club, where he can wear it when on site. The other award is the Champion's Medallion, a tradition which started with Ben Hogan's first victory in 1951. All previous winners and those since have been given the 2.3 ounce, 14-carat gold coin which is die-struck on each side and measures 1¾ inches in diameter. The medallion features the champion's name and year of victory on one side beneath the tournament logo.

The us Open

The original trophy — first won by Horace Rawlins at Newport Golf Club in Rhode Island in 1895 — and made of sterling silver, stood the test of time for only half a century. From the start, the USGA initiated a tradition where the champion golfer took the trophy to his home club for a year before returning it for the following year's championship. However, the original two-handled trophy with its distinctive hand-chased golfing scene was destroyed by fire in September 1946 at Lloyd Mangrum's home club, Tam O'Shanter, outside Chicago. The USGA considered replacing it with a new design, but opted instead to preserve the look of the original with a full-scale replica.

This replacement — complete with a winged female figure atop the bowl — remained in service and passed from champion to champion until 1986, when it was permanently retired to the USGA Museum. Nowadays the US Open champion takes custody of a full-scale replica for one year.

The Open

Its official name is the Golf Champion Trophy, but it is more commonly known as the Claret Jug. It is probably the most famed trophy in golf. The original was made by Mackay Cunningham & Company of Edinburgh and hallmarked 1873. The first Open champion to receive the trophy was Tom Kidd, but Young Tom Morris's name was the first to be engraved on it as the 1872 winner, at which point the trophy wasn't ready for presentation.

Following Bobby Jones's win in the 1927 Open, the R&A — who are responsible for the running of the championship — took the decision to retain the Claret Jug at St Andrews and to present the winner with a replica. In 1928, Walter Hagen won the third of his four Open titles and accepted the replica, having previously won the original in 1922 and 24.

As well as receiving a replica of the Claret Jug, the winner of the Open each year is presented with a Gold Medal. Up to the 1929 championship, the winner had to pay for the minting of the medal. But that practice ceased from 1930 onwards. Walter Hagen, the 1929 champion, was the last player to have the cost deducted from his prize money.

The US PGA

Known as the Wanamaker trophy — it was denoted by Rodman Wanamaker, a New York department store owner, in time for the inaugural championship in 1916 — it is, quite comfortably, the largest of all the Major trophies. It weighs 27 lbs, stands 28 inches high and has a width, from handle to handle, of 27 inches.

The trophy has often had an adventurous outing. Walter Hagen won four successive PGAS from 1924 to 27 but lost in the quarter-finals of 1928. When asked to return the trophy, he informed the PGA of America that it was missing. Hagen said he entrusted the trophy to a taxi driver to take to his hotel after winning the 1927 event in Dallas and that it never arrived. In 1930 the trophy was found by accident. A porter cleaning the cellar of a warehouse in Detroit found the Wanamaker trophy sealed in a leather case. The warehouse was owned by the Walter Hagen Golf Company.

Nowadays the champion does not get to keep the actual Wanamaker trophy. The PGA of America offers a scaled-down replica, approximately half the original size, at no cost to the champion.

Chapter 2 ∿

. . . AND OUT OF THE WILDERNESS!

Little could he have known it at the time, but Fred Daly's win in the 1947 British Open at Royal Liverpool Golf Club, or Hoylake as it is more commonly known, became something of a monkey on the backs of Irish tour professionals for decades afterwards.

Try as they might, the quest for a Claret Jug — for the championships in the United States were, quite literally, another world for most of Ireland's professionals — proved to be an elusive one. Christy O'Connor Snr played his first Open in 1951, at Royal Portrush, and proved to be a perennial contender: he had no fewer than 10 career top-10 finishes in the Major with a best finish of tied-third at Royal Lytham & St Annes in 1958, when Australian Peter Thomson triumphed.

Harry Bradshaw, one of Senior's closest friends, had an even closer call. In the 1949 championship at Sandwich, Bradshaw lost in a play-off to the great South African Bobby Locke. However, it was generally felt that Bradshaw should have been entitled to relief in his second round when his drive landed up against a broken beer bottle by the fifth fairway. Rather than taking a drop, Bradshaw opted to play the ball as it lay and only moved it a matter of inches. It was to make all the difference in the end.

Others too had their moments in attempting to emulate Daly
— who had birdied the 72nd hole to claim a one-stroke winning
margin over Reg Horne and the amateur Frank Stranahan at
Hoylake — but, for years, all came up short. Des Smyth was tied-
fourth in 1982 at Royal Troon; Christy O'Connor Jnr, a nephew of
his namesake, finished tied-third behind Sandy Lyle at Sandwich
in 1985; Eamonn Darcy was tied-fifth behind Ian Baker Finch at
Royal Birkdale in 1991; and David Feherty flirted with contention
in Turnberry in 1994, but eventually finished fourth behind Nick
Price.

Of the newer generation, Darren Clarke had seemed to be the
one most likely to make the breakthrough in emulating his fellow-
Royal Portrush member. With a game honed on the fine links
courses of north Antrim, Clarke contended in the 1997 Open at
Troon (where he finished runner-up to Justin Leonard) and the
2001 championship at Royal Lytham & St Annes (where he
finished tied-third behind David Duval).

Finally, when the time came for deliverance, it was Pádraig
Harrington who ended the drought. Exactly 60 years after Daly
became the first Irishman to win a Major, Harrington — the
youngest of five golfing brothers — made the breakthrough. Not
only that, but his maiden win at Carnoustie in 2007 was followed
by a successful defence of the Claret Jug at Royal Birkdale in 2008,
and then a win at the 2008 US PGA Championship at Oakland Hills.

What's more, Harrington's victory seemed to open the flood-
gates. Where Daly had shown the way all those years before,
Harrington became the modern pioneer. Graeme McDowell
followed him in the Majors club with a victory in the 2010 US

Open at Pebble Beach. Rory McIlroy won the 2011 US Open at Congressional Country Club in Maryland, outside Washington DC. And, not to be outdone, Clarke — finally and somewhat belatedly — got his due reward for years of endeavour when he landed the 2011 Open at Sandwich.

You only have to walk into the golf clubs that produced Ireland's golden generation of Major champions to realise how revered they are by their own. In Harrington's case, an entire room — quite appropriately known as the 'Harrington Room' — at Stackstown Golf Club in the foothills of the Dublin mountains has been elegantly transformed into a museum of sorts. There, along with trophies, photographs, newspaper articles and flags, his path from young amateur to multiple Major champion has been chronicled.

The walls at Holywood Golf Club in north Down are adorned with evidence of McIlroy's path to Major success, including a framed copy of the newspaper article that told of his win in the World Juniors (age group 9–10) in Doral. McDowell gave a replica of his US Open trophy to his home club, Rathmore. And Clarke gave his Gold Medal for winning the Open to Royal Portrush, where — appropriately — it has been proudly placed alongside Daly's.

———

The success of Irish golfers since Harrington's first Major win has been quite phenomenal. It is worth putting into context: there were 17 Majors from the 2007 Open at Carnoustie to the 2011

Open at Sandwich. Irish golfers won six of them, a strike-rate unmatched by any other golfing nation. After Ireland's six, the next best was five by the superpower that is the United States, followed by South Africa (three), Germany (one), South Korea (one) and Argentina (one).

How did Ireland get from a position of glorying for so long in only one Major champion — Fred Daly — to the point where it has bred a succession of them? When McIlroy won his US Open title at Congressional, the then world No. 1 Luke Donald wistfully tweeted that he was considering a move to the new golfing capital of the world: Northern Ireland. If only it were so easy.

Without a doubt, this generation of Irish golfers has proven itself to be a golden one. Was it by accident, or design? Was it a case of hugely talented players all coming off the conveyor belt at the same time?

What is beyond any doubt is that the Golfing Union of Ireland (GUI), the organisation which controls amateur golf on an all-island basis, deserved whatever kudos came their way. The GUI has developed a state-of-the-art facility at its base in Carton House in Maynooth, Co. Kildare, which — along with the Ulster Branch's own academy in Greenmount, Co. Antrim — has enabled talented young golfers to work on their games with back-up assistance from coaches, nutritionists and physical therapists.

Clarke was the one many envisioned leading the way if any Irish player was to win a Major. As it turned out, he became a follower. 'Pádraig won three Majors in very quick succession and that pushed all of the rest of us guys on. No disrespect to Pádraig, but if Pádraig can do it, others feel they can do it. Pádraig has led the way and then we have all come along behind.

'In the whole process of golf in Ireland, we are unbelievably lucky to have so many talented players. For a very small country in terms of golf and golfing talent, we are almost at the top of that league. And because our pool is so small, compared to places like America, we've got some of the very best players in the world. We're very fortunate.'

Clarke has done his own thing in assisting the GUI to nurture talent. His Darren Clarke Foundation has taken the very best young boys and girls from all over Ireland to a finals weekend, where the golfer has also provided clinics. He has also, in association with the GUI's Ulster Branch, initiated the Darren Clarke School — for those aspiring to careers in the golf industry, including a possible future as tour players — at the campus in Greenmount.

McIlroy cut his teeth as an amateur and benefited hugely from the GUI system before going on to greater heights as a professional, winning a first Major at the 2011 US Open and getting to the world No. 1 position on a number of occasions in 2012. Of the impact made by Irish players on the biggest of stages, McIlroy observed: 'The GUI have been a big part of it. I don't know if any other golf union in the world has a set-up like Carton House . . . They just keep producing players.'

When the GUI was in the process of developing a National Academy at Carton House, Harrington was approached to advise on what should be included. Typically, there were no half-measures from Harrington, who nit-picked down to the type of grasses that should be used in the short game area.

'I think professional (tour) golfers now, and the GUI has got much more to grips with this, tend to come from the amateur ranks, whereas (the generation) before us tended to come from the PGA club professional ranks. There's great stories of, say, David Feherty who was a four-handicapper in the pro shop (going out on tour) . . . Now the GUI will train young amateur golfers to leave them,' said Harrington.

More than that, many of those who evolved through the GUI set-up — or, as McDowell did, through a scholarship system in the United States — took Irish golf to new heights. No longer was the benchmark set at keeping a tour card or winning on the PGA European Tour. Harrington proved, and others followed, in believing that Major victories were possible.

A pertinent point made by Harrington in his analysis of why Ireland produced so many good players, was the quality of the courses. 'Our (weather) conditions obviously produce players who can work their way around a golf course, but you do also have to give credit to the golf clubs who run tournaments — the West of Ireland at Rosses Point, the North at Royal Portrush, the different Scratch Cups, real competitive golf. I know as a kid I could travel the length and breadth of the country. When you didn't have school, there was always a golf tournament on or a scratch cup, something to go to. I don't think there is another country that offers that.'

When the R&A's Peter Dawson considered the question of Ireland's series of Major triumphs, he settled on this reply: 'I think these things go in cycles, and Ireland clearly has had some very, very talented players. I think if you examine them, they've all come through slightly different routes probably to get to where they are, so you can't put your finger on one particular method. But each of them has talent and application, and those are the essential ingredients.' Dawson added: 'I'd be exaggerating if I said I saw something in the Irish coaching system that was causing it. I simply don't know.'

For sure, the Golfing Union of Ireland — which fosters talent at provincial level through each of its four branches in Ulster, Leinster, Connacht and Munster, and also at national level — would appear to have ticked all the necessary boxes in developing players, nurturing them and then releasing them into a world where they not only play for pay but, as we've seen, go on to win Major titles.

And yet, if you take the three Ulster players who followed up on Harrington's trailblazing of 2007 and 2008 when the Dubliner won three Majors in little over 13 months, it is fair to acknowledge that they have, as Dawson put it, 'come through slightly different routes'.

Take the first two winners, for example. McDowell — the 2010 US Open champion — pursued a collegiate route, heading to the University of Alabama where he learnt the art of winning (on the college circuit where he broke the stroke average record of one Tiger Woods, and then on his summer visits back home where he amassed a collection of provincial and national titles) before turning to life as a pro.

McIlroy's route was different and swifter, having won the Irish Close as a 15-year old and the European Amateur a year later in 2006. The Walker Cup at Royal Co. Down in 2007 was hardly over, by which time, and still a teenager, he made a natural move into the paid ranks.

After his US Open win at Congressional, McIlroy was asked why so many Irish players were winning Majors. 'I think it starts with the people, (that) golf is very accessible. There's obviously a lot of great golf courses. And a big help to me growing up was the Golfing Union of Ireland and the help that they gave me through- out my junior career and amateur career, enabling me to go and play in different places around the world. To learn about different conditions, different cultures, it really prepared me for coming out on Tour.'

What McDowell and McIlroy had in common was the GUI's policy of sending them abroad to play in tournaments which became an important part of their development. Elite players were sent to continental Europe and as far afield as Australia to sharpen their competitive instincts. Another common denominator was that they learnt how to win, and amassed titles around the island of Ireland and abroad which created a winning culture in their minds which remains to this day.

Where the two differed was that McIlroy chose to stay at home, whereas McDowell opted to take the collegiate route to the United States. 'I'm a big fan of the collegiate system, especially for kids in the UK and Ireland who are making the transition (from school) when all they want to do is play golf and want to hit the pro ranks and they're maybe not quite ready. I generally try and point them in the direction of the American college system, to try and keep their eye on the academic side and to play two, three, four years of quality competitive golf. There's no doubt it was the turning point in my career, the three years I spent (at the University of Alabama). I came as a decent player and left ready for the pro ranks. I think it is the best system in the world as far as getting guys ready from that 18 through to 22-year-old bracket where they're in no-man's land, where they have to leave junior golf and not quite ready for senior level.'

When Clarke turned professional in 1990 — deciding not to wait around for the 1991 Walker Cup in Portmarnock the following year — there was a firm belief at the time that his talent was such that he would become the first Irishman to win a Major championship since Daly had lifted the Claret Jug in 1947. Who would have believed that three different players from Ireland would have won five Majors before Clarke finally managed to get his hands on one? Perhaps that long wait made it all the sweeter?

There is another common denominator apparent in the cases of Harrington, Clarke, McDowell and McIlroy, and that is the role their parents played in encouraging them in their chosen sport. Harrington literally lived in the shadow of his late father Paddy, a former All-Ireland football finalist with his native Cork, who saw Stackstown Golf Club as a home away from home and who brought his young son there day-in and day-out where his golfing passion was nurtured.

Likewise, Godfrey Clarke, who had himself played Irish League soccer with Glenavon and Dungannon Swifts and also rugby with Dungannon, told of how he and his wife Hettie had taken out family membership at Dungannon Golf Club for £112 and of how a young Darren would be dropped to the course with a packed lunch and a couple of pounds and would often play 54 holes a day.

'We all did it . . . Gerry and Rosie (with Rory), Kenny and Marian (with Graeme). We all did that. We came from an ordinary working-class family, but you have to give him a chance. If you didn't, you'd be thinking later on in life, why not? He has repaid us in full since, let's put it that way,' explained Godfrey of the sacrifices made in ensuring their son got to develop in his formative playing years. Clarke's father added: 'We always hoped it would (see him win a Major). Everybody hopes something like this comes along. He totally deserves it, that's all I'm saying.'

The role which Clarke has played in nurturing young players should not be overlooked. The Darren Clarke Foundation is aimed at developing junior players all over Ireland — complementing the work of the GUI — and McIlroy was one of those players to benefit from Clarke's influence and mentoring. Apart from the Foundation, there is also the Darren Clarke Golf School based at the Greenmount campus in Antrim, beside the Ulster branch of the GUI.

Asked if he saw the Darren Clarke Foundation as his legacy, Clarke responded: 'Well, legacy is not really something that I think about an awful lot, but I just want the kids to have a good time that are involved in my foundation. I want them to enjoy the game, whatever form that may come in, whether it be a short game clinic, whether it be a weekend where they're working hard on their games. All my stuff is to try to help the kids in whatever shape or fashion I can.

'You know, as well as my Foundation, I have my school in Antrim where I pop in and try (to help). My whole outlook on the game has come full circle where I'm trying to give back because the game has been very kind to me over a long period of time, so I'm trying to help the kids in any way I can.'

———

Of Ireland's four modern-day Major champions, McIlroy — a golfing phenomenon from a young age — took less time than the others to make the grade. His, it would seem, has been a seamless journey, from capturing amateur titles in Rosses Point, Westport and the European Club, to conquering golf on a global stage.

Those who know McIlroy most closely of all are the ones least surprised by his rise to greatness. 'He's great for golf, a breath of fresh air,' said McDowell, who preceded his fellow-Ulsterman as the US Open champion. 'Perhaps we're ready for golf's next super-star and perhaps Rory is it.'

There's something about Rory that is special, for sure. Even Jack Nicklaus, the greatest Major champion of them all, developed a soft spot for him. More than a soft spot, in fact. The Golden Bear took McIlroy under his wing after the 2011 final round collapse at the Masters and gave him advice on how to rebound.

The McIlroy-Nicklaus contact first came about by chance. Nicklaus tells the story of driving into a shopping mall in Palm Beach Gardens during the 2009 Honda Classic, a week after McIlroy had made his debut on the US Tour at the WGC-Accenture Match Play. Nicklaus spotted the courtesy car and then noticed the mop of curly hair and knew who it was. 'Hi,' he said to Rory, 'I thought that was you.'

That chance encounter developed into a relationship that transcended the generation gap. Nicklaus invited McIlroy to use the practice area at his private club, the Bear's Club, in Florida.

When McIlroy returned to the area for the 2010 Honda Classic, Nicklaus invited McIlroy to lunch. It developed into a 90-minute talk from master to pupil on how to become a Major champion. Nicklaus — with 18 — knew how to win better than anyone. But, as a 19-time runner-up, he had also learnt about losing. His insight was, McIlroy recalled, 'an unbelievable experience'.

One of the experiences which Nicklaus recounted to the young Irishman involved the British Open at Turnberry in 1977, where the final round — the so-called 'Duel in the Sun' — became a two-man battle between Nicklaus and Tom Watson. 'He told me that the best he has ever played was in the Open at Turnberry and yet Tom Watson won.'

After McIlroy's collapse in the 2011 Masters, where he carried a four-stroke lead into the final round but eventually fell like a stone to finish 15th after one calamitous play after another on the back nine, Nicklaus sought him out.

The meeting came at the 2011 Memorial tournament, an event hosted by Nicklaus. What was said? 'He said to me, I'm expecting big things from you,' recalled McIlroy. 'It's a nice pressure to have knowing that the greatest player ever thinks that you're going to do pretty good. He said he always put a lot of pressure on himself. He expected to play well. He expected to be up there all the time in a position to win. And he said, I expect you to do the same thing.'

In a way, McIlroy fed that same vibe on to Clarke. After McIlroy won the US Open at Congressional, Clarke withdrew from the scheduled PGA European Tour event — the BMW International Open in Munich, Germany — so that he could partake in the party festivities back in Belfast. Over a few drinks, McIlroy effectively told Clarke to get the finger out and that it was time for him to win a Major.

The success of the three Northern Irishmen in winning three Majors in the space of 13 months from June 2010 to July 2011 was extraordinary. 'The probability of Northern Ireland producing back-to-back US Open champions is a lottery number, bigger than that,' remarked McDowell after McIlroy followed him into the winner's enclosure in America's national championship.

How did he explain it? 'It's just watching your colleagues and friends and guys you play with week in and week out doing things. It gives people belief,' said McDowell.

McDowell and McIlroy were not alone in making Major breakthroughs. The South Africans, Louis Oosthuizen and Charl Schwartzel, also fed off each other: Oosthuizen was hugely impressive in winning the 2010 British Open at St Andrews and Schwartzel birdied the last four holes, unprecedented in the history of the Masters, to win his Green Jacket in 2011. The American, Keegan Bradley, also showed that he was up to the task when he captured the US PGA at Atlanta Country Club in 2011 — all young players, all fearless.

One of the reasons why so many first-time Major champions emerged in that period was that the aura of invincibility once held by Tiger Woods had dissipated. Another reason was that the young players — many of whom grew up emulating Woods, bringing a fitness programme and technical awareness with them into their chosen careers — were just very good.

As McDowell put it, 'I think the 21st-century golfer is a lot more ready for the Tour. The younger players are so much more ready for the Tour when they come out. They play professional events. They know how to win. And they're not scared any more. I think golfers are tougher and better and the standard is so much better across the board, and technology has maybe levelled the playing field a little bit as well.'

———

When Ben Hogan won the British Open at Carnoustie in 1953, 'The Hawk' returned to a ticker-tape parade in New York. When he got home to Fort Worth in Texas, another celebratory parade along the streets awaited him.

In 2007, when Pádraig Harrington ended the 60-year drought since Fred Daly's Major win, the Dubliner didn't get such a reception. There was no open-top bus tour of the city's streets, no ticker-tape. What he got was a State reception in Leinster House — the Irish Houses of Parliament — where the taoiseach of the time, Bertie Ahern, played host to the golfer.

By the time Harrington was invited to the White House in Washington DC in 2010, he had become a multi-Major champion and, in the spirit of the occasion, he brought with him a specially commissioned set of left-handed clubs, supplied by his sponsor Wilson, for President Barack Obama.

Unfortunately for Harrington, he never got to shake hands with the United States President that day. However, when President Obama made a visit to Ireland in 2011 — visiting his ancestral home in Moneygall, Co. Offaly — Harrington was among those who shared a VIP stage with the great and the good of Irish society in welcoming him. And, on that occasion, Harrington did more than just meet President Obama: he gave him an impromptu golf lesson backstage.

Harrington's rise to become one of golf's international superstars by virtue of his Major triumphs was one, it seemed, that took him by surprise more than anyone. After all, he had delayed any notion of turning professional — at the relatively late age of 21 — until he had completed his accountancy qualifications. 'I decided to turn pro because the guys I was able to beat as an amateur were turning pro, not because I thought I was good enough. I thought I would have a great life. And if I did well, maybe I'd make a comfortable living on the Tour. The idea was to turn pro, have a couple of years on the Tour if I could, learn the ropes and see what I needed to do to improve.'

Such limited ambitions changed fairly quickly. Harrington won the Spanish Open in Madrid in his rookie season. He had been a pro for just 10 weeks. 'I started so well I just kept my head down and ran with it. I couldn't really believe how well I did. It was fairytale stuff,' he recalled.

The 1997 US Open was held at Congressional Country Club — when South African Ernie Els ran out a one-stroke winner over Scotland's Colin Montgomerie — and Harrington left somewhat battered and bruised by the experience. 'It was just too difficult for me. I couldn't get around a golf course like that. I shot 76, 77 and came home thinking, well, I'm a good golfer, but that's really tough unless I do something about it.'

It was then that Harrington started working with veteran Scottish coach Bob Torrance and the tireless and relentless quest to work on his game started in earnest. The focus was to make his game more suitable for US-style golf courses, where a high ball flight was necessary. The irony was that his breakthrough Major win came on the type of seaside links course that he had spent his amateur days competing in the length and breadth of Ireland.

As Harrington's game evolved, he started getting into contention in the Majors. In the 2002 British Open at Muirfield, he had a chance of winning (he finished a stroke outside a play-off won by Els). And in the 2006 US Open at Winged Foot, he had also got into contention on the home stretch, only to come up short with a couple of late bogeys.

When the hard questions were asked of him at Carnoustie in 2007, Harrington — a seasoned player in the Majors — answered them in the most emphatic manner. Of that play-off win over Sergio García, he remarked: 'I drew on all my experience of playing links golf and convinced myself I was going to win.'

That ability to convince himself that he was going to win was one that, over time, had served other great players — Gary Player, Jack Nicklaus, Seve Ballesteros, Nick Faldo. At the time of that maiden Major victory on the eastern coast of Scotland, Harrington — or anyone else — couldn't have known that it was just the start of great things for Irish golf. The drought was well and truly over.

Ireland's four modern-day Major champions are very much involved in charitable causes. Three of them — Pádraig Harrington, Darren Clarke and Graeme McDowell — have their own Foundations, and Rory McIlroy has a position as ambassador with UNICEF.

THE DARREN CLARKE FOUNDATION

Darren Clarke established his Foundation in 2002 with a number of aims: to give children, who might not otherwise have the opportunity, to play golf, and to pass on his knowledge and experience to elite young players. He targeted boys and girls who were already making a name for themselves in junior golf and came up with the idea of hosting a Champions' Weekend — staged at Portmarnock Golf Club and Portmarnock Links — each year. 'It is very satisfying to see the level and depth of talent that exists in Irish junior golf and I see a visible increase in the standards with each year that passes,' said Clarke.

Apart from assisting promising young players with bursaries, the Darren Clarke Foundation also raises funds for Breast Cancer Awareness. Clarke's first wife Heather died of the disease in 2006.

THE PADRAIG HARRINGTON FOUNDATION

Pádraig Harrington established his Foundation to provide financial assistance to deserving beneficiaries. 'With a wonderful family, I feel extremely privileged to be in the position I am in. How many of us get paid to do something we love so much? I do appreciate, however, that there are others who are less fortunate,' he said.

Apart from his Foundation, Harrington is also a global ambassador for the Special Olympics, a supporter of Make A Wish Ireland and a patron of the third world charity GOAL.

THE G-MAC FOUNDATION

Graeme McDowell established his Foundation in 2011 to support children's medical research in Northern Ireland, the Republic of Ireland and the United States. In addition to raising funds for research in children's medicine, the Foundation annually brings a group of children from Ireland to Florida for 'the holiday of a lifetime'. McDowell has also been a long-term supporter of Multiple Sclerosis charities, a cause that remains a priority in his charitable work. 'Charity is something I've always wanted to be involved in. There are so many good, deserving causes out there, but I think you have to focus on a few to make a meaningful difference.'

Chapter 3

THE CLARET JUG, LADYBIRDS, AND THE END OF THE DROUGHT . . .

136th Open Championship, Carnoustie,
Scotland

July 2007

T wo men, one graced with charisma and the other with a sense of his own importance, strode into Carnoustie Golf Club — an unpretentious building located on a road called Links Parade and across the way from the rather grander structure of the hotel and championship links — on the Monday morning of 16 July 2007. Pádraig Harrington, still in bed and mildly concerned about a neck strain, wasn't aware that Seve Ballesteros and Nick Faldo, donned in waterproofs that morning to combat the miserable weather, were earmarked for a breakfast briefing with a small number of golf writers or what would come from the chat around an oval table.

Harrington was having a rare lie-in, and nursing a slight neck injury that surfaced after winning the Irish PGA Championship at the European Club in Brittas Bay two days previously. It would be a day when he wouldn't bother to hit a ball. Rest and physiotherapy was the key to his recovery, and the manner of his win over the links in Co. Wicklow the previous week — when most tour players competed in the Barclays Scottish Open on the manicured parkland course of Loch Lomond — had him in no doubt that his game was in good shape.

In his mind, by opting to play competitive links golf in the Irish PGA, he had stolen a march on the field gathering on the north-east coast of Scotland for the third Major of the year.

It would only be later, through the bush telegraph operated by the caddies on the range and in the caddy shack, that word would filter around the course playing host to the 136th Open Championship that Mr Faldo's breakfast chat over coffee and croissants included an accusation that the current generation of European players were, in his mind, 'too chummy'. He didn't quite say too soft, but that was the underlying inference.

Who could say he was wrong? It had been in this same part of the world, way back in 1999, when Paul Lawrie came from nowhere to win the Open. On that occasion, conditions were so poor, with the rough horrifically high, that the venue was renamed 'Carnasty' by players and caddies alike. Since then, no fewer than 31 Major championships had been staged on either side of the Atlantic without any European player managing to emulate Lawrie's triumph. Faldo was right, much as the litany of losing statistics may have irked those Europeans aspiring to a Major title win.

In backing up those facts with his own observations, Faldo didn't hold back. 'It's very different from our era to this era. We were competitors and we were very separate individuals. I always believed you kept your cards close to your chest. Now, the modern guys all have lunch together and then go off to play for a million dollars. And I think, hmmm, I can't imagine sitting down with Seve (Ballesteros) or Greg (Norman) or Pricey (Nick Price) before we go out. It all seems very different now.'

Faldo went on: 'It's very interesting, they all seem to be so much more chummy. Tiger (Woods) would be the one exception. He won't give away any secrets. He's a fierce competitor and I think that is the difference. We weren't the lads. We were all individuals. Now it seems like they are the lads. Me, Seve, (Bernhard) Langer, (Sandy) Lyle, Woosie (Ian Woosnam). And, I mean, Ollie (José María Olazábal) stepped into that group as well . . . Look what we achieved. Need I say more? There's 18 Majors between six guys. That's 18 Majors to . . . zero!'

It seemed only natural that Harrington would be one of those quizzed on his reactions to Faldo's assertion that the new generation of European golfer simply didn't match up to those who went before them, at least when it came to winning Majors. Harrington hadn't entered the professional game with the same hoopla that accompanied the likes of, say, Sergio García or Luke Donald, but in his near 12 years on the road he had evolved and matured into one of the world's top players, albeit one still without a Major to his name!

As boxing folk might say, Harrington arrived in Carnoustie as a contender. There were a number of reasons for this: one, he had twice won the Alfred Dunhill Links Championship in the previous four years, a PGA European Tour event played annually in this neck of the woods and which included Carnoustie on its rota; two, he had got one monkey off his back by winning the Irish Open at Adare Manor in May, ending a 25-year drought since the last Irish player won it, John O'Leary; and three, he had served his time in the Majors. Indeed, Harrington had finished just one stroke outside a play-off in the Open of 2002 at Muirfield when Ernie Els emerged as the champion.

One other thing stood in Harrington's favour going into the British Open at Carnoustie that summer. He had played in and won the Irish PGA Championship at the European — an event set up on Pat Ruddy's masterpiece to replicate the tough conditions of Carnoustie — where he rediscovered the craft of shot-making on links terrain and delved into his reserves to beat Brendan McGovern, a stubborn club professional with his sights set on taking down the top dog, in extra holes. So he was battle-hardened. Focused. Confident.

On Tuesday, having taken a break from practice the previous day to alleviate his niggling neck injury, Harrington was asked to respond to Faldo's inferences that the current crop of Europeans simply didn't match up to the old guys. As is his way, Harrington's reply provided an interesting insight into his own world. 'We all have different ways of going about things . . . Just because you're a nice guy, it doesn't mean you can't win a Major. You have to have an instinct to win. But nice guys do win!'

Just as Faldo had done things his way, so too would Harrington. In fact, the evidence that Harrington would stick to his own guns and, as Faldo might have put it, be chummy, was provided on the Wednesday of that week. It was customary to see Harrington and his fellow-Dubliner Paul McGinley head out together in the practice days before a tournament, and the eve of the 136th British Open was no exception.

Theirs was a friendship which had developed with time.

Although both players hailed from the same suburb of Rathfarnham in south Dublin, had played Gaelic football for the same club (Ballyboden St Enda's) and had even played on the same Walker Cup team — at Portmarnock in 1991 — there was a near five-year age gap between them and their real bonding had taken place after the pair won the World Cup for Ireland at Kiawah Island in 1997.

In the light of the pre-championship comments from Faldo, it was a tad ironic that Harrington had only recently gone out of his way to get McGinley working with Dr Bob Rotella, the famed sports psychologist who had been his own mind guru for the best part of a decade. To Harrington, friendship was as important as any rivalry. If he could help McGinley, then he would.

On Wednesday, Harrington and McGinley embarked on their final practice run over the links by bypassing the first hole and commencing on the second, a par 4 of 463 yards that had a sand trap — known as Braid's Bunker — positioned in the middle of a fairway that curved gently to the right. For the first few holes, anyone watching wouldn't have been too excited by Harrington's form. Far from it in fact. He parred the second, bogeyed the third and then on the fourth did an impression of the man from the Hamlet ad where he found a fairway bunker and ran up a quadruple bogey.

The disaster, albeit one incurred on a practice day, seemed to give Harrington a kick up the backside. From the fifth to the ninth holes, he had two birdies and three pars. Then he set off the fireworks. Over the following seven holes, Harrington had a run of birdie-birdie-par-birdie-eagle-birdie-birdie. Players don't normally like to waste birdies or eagles on practice rounds or in regular pre-tournament pro-ams, but Harrington went to bed on the eve of the championship in good fettle.

He probably felt, too, that he was due a good performance in the British Open. After that near-miss in 2002, when he finished in fifth position but just one shot outside a four-way play-off, Harrington's subsequent performances saw him finish 22nd in 2003, miss the cut in 2004, fail to play in 2005 due to the death of his father, and then miss the cut again in 2006.

Yet, there was a sense of expectancy about Harrington's participation at Carnoustie. There was a feeling that he had served his time. Harrington was generally available at odds of 22/1 with the bookmakers but, putting on his numbers hat, the qualified account-ant remarked ahead of the championship: 'I wouldn't accept it's my best chance of winning. Sure, I look forward to coming here. But I can't have that ultimatum in my head that this is my best chance. That's going to put too much expectation on the week, too much focus on the week. I just have to keep working on a numbers game, to keep playing and to keep getting myself into contention. Just because I've won here before (in the Dunhill), I can't say it is my big chance. By having an attitude like that will only put more pressure on you. The key is to tone it down all the way, and just play yourself into position with nine holes to go on Sunday.'

———

The task of compiling a score in a Major, any Major, is when the men are sorted out from the boys. Nobody had to remind Sergio García of this. In 1999, as a 19-year old setting out on his golfing

odyssey, García shot a second round 89 in the Open championship on the brutally tough links and, rather cruelly, those
competitors who embarked on their respective missions in the
first round of the 136th Open were given a visual reminder of the
young Spaniard's experience.

A series of photographs from the 1999 Open lined the wall of
the hotel corridor close by the first tee and the 18th green. One
photograph, in particular, offered a graphic reminder of
Carnoustie's capacity to inflict carnage on players. It showed the
scoreboard of one group having completed the second round. It
read: 'Singh +19 Mediate +13 García +30.' García had finished
bottom of the pile and had made a tearful departure in the arms
of his mother wondering why the golfing gods should inflict such
a fate on him.

On the morning of 19 July 2007, the first players to be welcomed on to the first tee for a 6.30 am tee time were Joe Durant,
an American who didn't bother to don any waterproofs despite a
steady rainfall, Oliver Wilson and Ben Bunny. It would be almost
seven hours later, at 1.20 pm, that Ivor Robson, the official starter,
would call Pádraig Harrington to the tee to commence his own
personal journey in the quest for the famed Claret Jug.

Much happened on that first day, but nothing as beguiling as
the wizardry exhibited by García. Eight years on from his
nightmare, he returned to the scene of his humiliation and found
a form of redemption. García — the player expected to carry on
the Major-winning exploits of the legendary Seve Ballesteros and
José María Olazábal — opened with a 65, six-under-par, that gave
him the first round lead.

Naturally enough, García was all smiles after his 65 provided the highlight of an opening day which also witnessed the arrival on the world stage of a young amateur from Northern Ireland. Rory McIlroy, in the field as the European Individual Amateur champion, produced a bogey-free round of 68 that was one better than Tiger Woods. 'It's a pretty special feeling, to say that you were better than Tiger,' remarked McIlroy, who received a standing ovation on exiting the 18th green after his round.

Generally, it was a good day for the Irish players. McIlroy's 68 was sandwiched between a 67 from Paul McGinley and a 69 from Harrington.

But this was García's day, proof perhaps that the demons of 1999 had vanished. It would prove to be wishful thinking, but for the moment he was a happy man. He had missed the cut in both the US Masters and the US Open and arrived in Carnoustie wielding a belly-putter that tucked into his stomach and lessened the impact of his hands on the stroke.

The putter belonged to his father Victor, but came at the suggestion of Vijay Singh who had witnessed García's woes in 1999 when accompanying him for the first two rounds. This time there were smiles instead of tears as García recounted his decision to change to the long putter: 'Vijay has been telling me for a year or two (to switch), but I haven't been listening. When I feel comfortable with the short putter, I feel really good with it. But it seems to be highs and lows. I want to be more consistent. It feels like I can make a lot of putts with the belly.'

Reminded of his second round 89 on his last appearance over the links in an Open, García smiled and replied: 'This is not about revenge . . . I just want to play solid. This is a good start, definitely what the doctor ordered.'

Harrington, too, might have felt that an opening 69 was just what the doctor ordered. Although tied for eighth place and four shots adrift of García, Harrington finished the day on the same score as Woods despite not being entirely happy with his driver. He had broken his driver two weeks previously — playing a practice round on the eve of the Smurfit European Open at the K Club — and replaced it in his bag with an old driver with a 7.5° loft that he brought back to life. It would be one of two different drivers that Harrington used over the course of the four championship days, as he changed to a driver with an 8.5° loft over the weekend.

In that opening round of 69, Harrington's best shot, strangely enough, came early on and demonstrated both his mental strength and his ability to think outside the box. On the second hole he hit his approach shot into a greenside bunker and, upon reaching the trap, found the ball in a horrible lie right under the lip. Many players would have considered the option of taking an unplayable lie in the bunker, but he took a sand wedge from his caddie Ronan Flood, turned the face around backwards before playing out left-handed. The ball somehow found its way on to the putting surface and he was off and running.

Then on the 18th Harrington finished his round with another important shot. Again it was from a bunker. He hit a 48 yard bunker shot into the wind that nearly went in before spinning back to four feet. Afterwards, he was as pleased as punch with his start. 'I'm pleased with it. I've just got to do more of the same (for another three days) . . . I didn't drive the ball as well as I wanted to, so that is something to concern me.'

On that day, Harrington was only the third-best Irishman in the field. McGinley, who wore mittens throughout the course of his round to beat the cold, was the man closest to García. 'My Achilles heel is trying too hard, pushing too hard, playing too aggressively,' said McGinley, adding: 'Unless I'm playing well, patience is not one of my great traits. You have to let a score evolve and Pádraig is great at that. He is one of the best in the world at that.'

Harrington's advice to be more patient in his game benefited McGinley in that first round. But it would be Harrington's ability to use his own advice as the championship progressed that yielded the ultimate reward.

More often than not, a player must serve an apprenticeship in the Majors before becoming a champion. There are exceptions to the rule, most notably Ben Curtis who triumphed in the 2003 Open championship at Royal St George's in what was his first ever appearance in a Major. But, as García saved par on the 18th green of his second round, rolling in a putt for a 71 to add to his opening 65, there was a belief that his time had come. He had served whatever apprenticeship was required.

The smile as he left the 18th green told its own story, replacing the tears that had flowed when exiting the championship on the same links eight years previously. 'It was more of a grinder's day,' observed García of his day's work, which would leave him alone at the top of the midway leaderboard.

As it happened, one of those closely observing García's final act of the second round was Woods. The American was preparing to hit an iron — for safety — off the first tee. Shortly after García sank his par-saving putt on the last, Woods commenced his round with a swing that saw his ball hook left into the Barry Burn, the water hazard that snakes its way through the course. It led to a double-bogey six on Woods's opening hole of the second round and signalled that this would not be his time. He eventually signed for a second round 74 for 143, seven shots behind García.

On a day when a fresh breeze came in off the North Sea and the R&A chose some awkward pin placements to make scoring tougher (some 24 players had dipped below par in the first round), García's ability to avoid any disasters enabled him to reach the halfway stage on 136. South Korea's KJ Choi shot a 69 to move to 138 to become his nearest challenger, and Canadian Mike Weir's best-of-the-day 68 saw him move into a share of third place with Miguel Ángel Jiménez.

García, it must be said, had his moments. On the very first hole, from the middle of the fairway, he suffered a shank with just a nine-iron in his hand. His ball finished in tangled, heavy rough some 30 yards right of the green. It was there he showed his wizardry, taking a controlled swipe at the ball which floated over a greenside bunker and stopped 18 inches from the hole. That par save kept García, as he put it, in 'the right mood' to stay on course.

Not everyone remained immune from trouble. McIlroy, who would go on to win the Silver Medal as leading amateur, found the burn on the ninth where he took a double-bogey six *en route* to a 76 that left him sharing 31st place. More importantly, he survived the midway cut.

McGinley's magic of the first round also waned as he shot a second round 75 for 142. He ran up a double-bogey six on the third when he attempted to putt past a sprinkler head, as per European

Tour rules, and the ball jumped six inches off the ground. He only realised later he could have had a free drop under the R&A championship rules. He blamed nobody but himself for the oversight.

Harrington too had his woes. The 18th hole at Carnoustie — a par 4 of 499 yards and made infamous by Jean van de Velde's collapse in the 1999 Open — was to become the bane of Harrington's championship. In the second round, Harrington, right in the thick of the action, somehow ran up a double-bogey six after pushing his drive into the rough alongside the 17th fairway. It would be the last time that particular driver featured in the championship. From the lie, all he could do was lay up, playing back on to the 18th fairway, and then hit his approach to 20 feet. A couple of heavy-handed putts was followed by a tap-in.

Within minutes of signing his card for a 73 (level par 142), Harrington — whose sports psychologist Bob Rotella had stayed with him in the rented house in Carnoustie all week, a good move — had already erased the three-putt from his mind. The double-bogey had been forgotten. 'That six is not going to affect the outcome of this tournament for me. I don't want to be too far behind, but it just means that I go out and play good golf for the weekend. That's it,' said Harrington.

He added: 'There's a lot of golf left in this tournament and maybe I'll go out with a little more aggression from now on. There's 36 holes left and whether I'm one-under or two-under or level par, it doesn't make a difference to my chances on the weekend.'

Those words were to prove prophetic in their own way, but that second round was notable for one other thing: he played what he considered to be his 'shot of the week'. It came on the eighth hole, a par 3 of 183 yards, where he missed the green with his tee shot and was left with a dreadfully difficult shot off a tight lie over a yawning bunker. Harrington hit the ball to within 12 inches and moved on.

But García remained the man they all had to catch. 'I'd rather be leading than be eight shots back, that's for sure, because you don't feel like you have to push your game to the limit all the time,' said the Spaniard.

———

The third round of a tournament anywhere, be it the European Amateur or the Irish Close, a regular event on the PGA Tour or on the European Tour, is known as 'moving day'. It is the same deal in a Major championship, except with multiplied pressure. It seemed that García was immune to any such stress as he shot a bogey-free 68 for a 54-hole total of 204, which on Saturday evening saw him go to sleep with a three-shot lead over American Steve Stricker.

In fact, García seemed to be enjoying himself. Thoroughly enjoying himself. He probably won't have known anything about the stats of previous British Opens, which would have told him that only six champions in the history of the event had been outright leaders in every round: Ted Ray (1912), Bobby Jones (27), Gene Sarazen (32), Henry Cotton (34), Tom Weiskopf (73) and Tiger Woods (2005).

As it happened, the statistic most relevant to García was the one that told us that two players — Fred Daly (52) and Bobby Clampett (82) — had led for the first three rounds. And lost. Daly was joint-third in 52; Clampett joint-10th in 82.

García wasn't to know what fate would befall him on the Sunday, but on that Saturday evening he was by common consensus the heir apparent to the throne. Why not? For a third successive round the Spaniard played like a man who owned this piece of Scottish coastline. His shot-making was supreme, his putter was obedient, and his head was in the right place.

In the reshuffling that went on behind García in the third round, Stricker — who shot a course record-equalling 64 to be his closest pursuer — was the big mover, while there was a logjam of seven players, among them Harrington and McGinley, in a share of third place but all of six shots back.

Players heading out for the third round did so with a prediction of stormy weather on the horizon, remnants of a storm that had struck England the day before. The heavy rains never arrived, and the scoring — generally — had never been witnessed around Carnoustie in any previous Open. Stricker's 64 was the best of the lot, but 16 others recorded sub-70 scores.

Harrington had three birdies in his opening six holes, but couldn't buy a birdie on the way home. After bouncing back with a birdie on the 13th to offset the bogey on the 12th, he reeled off five successive pars to sign for a 68. He was six shots behind. Could he win? His demeanour after the round was one of complete and utter relaxation, outwardly at least. 'A nice return,' he acknowledged of his round, 'but not quite good enough to get right in there. It has left it in Sergio's hands . . . but I do feel I have a low round in me. I have to stay patient and let it happen.'

Unusually for somebody who had built a reputation as a range rat for his work ethic, with only Vijay Singh known to work as hard, Harrington — in an arrangement with his caddie Ronan

Flood — decided there was no need to hit the practice ground for any post-round work. The reasoning was simple: both Harrington and his caddie knew in their heart of hearts that he was playing well enough to win.

Instead of hitting the range, they headed back to Poppy House, normally a bed and breakfast in the town but taken over for the week by the Harrington family and entourage, where Harrington — over dinner — made what initially seemed to be a casual remark. 'I'm going to win,' he remarked. The comment was designed to illicit a reaction from his listeners, but it came out as more than that. It was part of the mental imagery that Rotella had encouraged him to put into the right side of his brain. 'I'm going to win. This is it,' he said

García probably went to bed nursing the same thoughts, believing that the demons of eight years previously would finally be exorcised. As he hit his pillow, García would have been wise to consider the advice once offered by Sir Winston Churchill to anyone who cared to listen. 'It is a mistake to look too far ahead. The chain of destiny can only be grasped one link at a time.'

———

Pádraig Harrington's day of destiny didn't start as planned, or how he would want it. He woke up to the sound of rain hitting the slated tiles but, more worryingly, with a strain in his neck. It had first reared its ugly head in the US PGA Championship in 2002, when his physical therapist Dale Richardson conducted remedial action on the first hole of the third round by grappling his man much as a wrestler would do to an opponent. The look on Harrington's face was one of sheer agony.

It was subsequently discovered that Harrington had a weakness around the C5 vertebrae and, over the ensuing years, had strengthened the muscles in the region through a tough physical regime. But there were times when the old injury flared up and, in terms of timing, this was definitely not what the doctor ordered. Having propped himself up with pillows, to limit any movement, Harrington managed to fall back into a sleep that didn't see him wake again until 10 o'clock, some four hours before his tee time in the third last group of the final round.

By the time Harrington got down to the breakfast table, his caddie Ronan Flood had already departed for the links to scout the final day's placements. Flood, a good amateur, had worked as a bank official with AIB Bank before leaving his desk behind to travel the world and the fairways with Harrington. It was to be a beneficial move for both player and bagman.

As he sat down to his breakfast, Harrington wondered why Jonny Smith, a family friend, was sitting at the table with a half-dozen golf balls. He knew Flood had already packed the customary dozen balls in his golf bag. Then it dawned on him: the balls were for a possible play-off. Flood had phoned back to Smith asking him to get another six balls in case they were required.

Flood's gesture of faith was appreciated by Harrington. It reminded him that Nick Faldo had come from six shots behind to beat Greg Norman in the 1996 US Masters, and that Paul Lawrie had come from 10 behind in the 1999 Open at Carnoustie. As Harrington tucked into his scrambled eggs and toast, he knew — as any big-time golfer knew — that, despite trailing García by six shots, the game was still alive. After all, only one other player, Stricker, separated the group in tied-third from the 54-hole leader. Someone could emerge from the pack. Why not him?

Before heading to the course, Harrington conducted a warm-up routine of stretching. The rented house was just five minutes from the links and Harrington timed his arrival — 12.15 pm — so that he could get a rub-down from his therapist Richardson, an Aussie who had built up his own small pool of players on tour. After almost 20 minutes of standard physiotherapy, and no recurrence of the neck spasm that had woken him in the early hours of the morning, Harrington headed to the range. It was 12.40 pm, plenty of time to stop on his way to sign autographs.

On the range Harrington hooked up with Flood and his coach Bob Torrance, who was like his shadow. He didn't worry too much about how he was hitting the ball, more about getting his head right. He felt good. He spent about half an hour on the range before he made his way to the short game area where he stuck to his routine and hit some bunker shots and some chip shots.

The next port of call was the putting green. All week, Harrington had spent no more than 10 minutes on the practice putting green before a round. It was an indication of how well he felt, how comfortable he was with the blade. He arrived on the green with 12 minutes to spare before his tee time, spent seven minutes hitting putts and then made his way to the first tee. Destiny called.

First things first, however. From the time he was a junior, being brought from one event to another by his father Paddy all around Ireland, Harrington had formed a habit on the first tee. It involved retying his shoe laces to ensure his shoes fitted properly.

Laced up, he turned to Flood and requested a five-wood. Just as he did so, there was a shift in the weather. For the first time that day, rays of sunshine broke through the grey clouds.

The overnight and morning rain had taken much of the sting out of the links and the assault by the players on the course was aided by some quite generous flag positions by the R&A. By the time Harrington teed off, other players had already proved that good scoring was possible. Ben Curtis, the 2003 champion, and Hunter Mahan signed for 65s. Richard Green, the Australian left-hander, went one better: he equalled the course record with a 64 that included a chip-in birdie on the ninth.

Despite Green's heroics, which eventually saw him finish in tied-fourth position, the real drama came afterwards. The central characters were to be Harrington and García, although the young Argentine Andrés Romero also played a leading role.

In golf there is nothing like the pressure experienced by a player in the final round of a Major. When García birdied the third hole to extend his lead to four shots, the smile on his face told its own story. It wasn't long afterwards, though, that the Spaniard discovered it wouldn't be all plain sailing. Far from it. On the fifth hole, García's tee shot came to a stop in an awkward lie on the edge of a bunker and he could only play back to the fairway. He ran up the first of three bogeys in a four-hole stretch. Suddenly, it was all to play for.

The surprise gatecrasher proved to be Romero, who conjured up a remarkable 10 birdies. Unfortunately for him, he also suffered two double-bogeys. The first of those came when his approach to the 12th green finished in a bush. Such a fate would have knocked the stuffing out of many a player. Not Romero. His response, quite incredibly, was to birdie the next four holes. Then disaster struck on the par 4 17th, where he got greedy with his second shot out of the rough. His two-iron shot was shanked into the wall of the Barry Burn and then, almost by a force of nature, ricocheted across the 18th fairway and past the out-of-bounds stakes. It led to a double-bogey six. He also bogeyed the 18th to sign for a 67, which left him on 278. It was the mark to beat.

Pádraig Harrington doesn't look at leaderboards. That's his caddie's job. He went into the final round with a game plan to chase birdies and covered the front nine in 33 strokes — claiming birdies at the third, sixth and eighth holes — to García's 38. As Harrington stood on the 11th tee, he was just one stroke behind García. When he birdied that hole, hitting an eight-iron to three feet, the overnight deficit of six shots had been erased. The chase was over and he was playing for a different, grander prize, the one he had dreamed about.

The Harrington-Flood team had first worked together in 2004, after the player surprisingly took the decision to end the six-year working relationship with David McNeilly. It was Flood's first caddying job, but he'd learnt the craft quickly. He was diligent and intelligent and, beyond the working relationship, there was a genuine friendship. Going out for the final round, the two had made a pact. There would be no looking at leaderboards, no up-dates to Harrington about who was doing what. They agreed that the first strategic decision would come on the par 5 14th: if Harrington needed birdies, Flood would hand him a driver; if he was in the thick of things, he would be given a five-wood.

Perhaps he already knew by the crowd's reaction to his birdie on the 11th that he was, indeed, in the thick of things. Flood passing the five-wood on the 14th tee confirmed it. A par 5 of 514 yards, it was a risk-and-reward hole and there was a feeling he was due a turn of fortune. On the 12th his birdie putt had lipped out. On the 13th another birdie putt stopped on the edge of the hole and stubbornly refused to drop.

On the 14th, his tee shot gave him the chance to go for the green in two. He did and, finally, he got a lucky bounce. In links golf there is a degree of luck. A good shot can kick into the rough after hitting the fairway. Bad luck. A slightly off-line shot can kick back into the fairway. Good luck. Harrington's approach landed in greenside rough but bounced and trickled on to the putting surface to 15 feet. He sank the eagle putt. 'Nothing had happened during the round to suggest it was my day until then. That was a big break,' he conceded.

Two matches behind, and listening to the roars from in front, García reacted by claiming back-to-back birdies on the 13th and 14th. They were both on nine-under. And when García's conservative play on the 15th hole backfired and resulted in a bogey, it meant that Harrington — who followed his eagle with a run of three pars — walked to the 18th tee box with a one-stroke lead.

What happened next was grotesque, unforgettable and yet riveting (for observers, if not for Harrington). He stood on the tee with a driver in his hand — one with an 8.5° loft that had been put into the bag on Saturday — and let fly with what he believed would be his last drive of the day. It was one of those moments in time that seemed to elapse in slow motion. The ball was pushed right, towards the burn that snaked its way up between the 18th and 17th holes, and ran across a pedestrian bridge before falling into the water hazard.

On his way to retrieve his ball, Harrington and García passed each other headed in opposite directions. 'Hello,' said García, smiling. Harrington simply nodded back. He couldn't get any words out.

On this same hole in the 1999 Open, Frenchman Jean van de Velde had run up a triple-bogey in losing his grip on the Claret Jug. He eventually lost out in a play-off to Paul Lawrie. And as Harrington took a penalty drop and chose to hit a five-iron for his third shot, with 207 yards to the front of the green and 229 yards to the flag, there was a look of sheer terror on his face after he caught it heavy and watched as the ball hit the ground and ran on into the burn.

'I was trying to get about 10 yards on the green. I was aiming at the out-of-bounds on the left in a right-to-left wind and trying to cut it in there. It was a difficult shot to take on and I hit a poor shot. I didn't execute it well. I hit it fat.'

It was a measure of Harrington's fortitude that he composed himself and, after taking his second penalty drop in the space of five minutes, hit a beautifully judged pitch shot that stopped five feet past the hole. 'The putt was the most pressure filled I had all day.' He rolled it in, and barely had time to think before his son Paddy was jumping into his arms. He didn't have time to think of what might have been.

That double-bogey six handed the initiative back to García. In the week where Ballesteros had formally announced his retirement from championship golf, it seemed as if the stars and planets were aligning to herald the young matador as the next champion. García was one shot up standing on the 18th tee, but chose a conservative play to take the out-of-bounds down the left and the burn to the right out of play. He left himself with 250 yards to the green, found a greenside bunker and then splashed out to 12 feet. He had a putt to win the Open. And, from the moment he hit it, it seemed perfect for pace and line. But it wasn't. It somehow missed. He was tied with Harrington after 72 holes. The Irishman had finished with a 67 for 277, seven-under; the Spaniard with a 73 for 277.

————

After completing his round, Pádraig Harrington had taken his young son into his arms and embraced his wife Caroline. He then headed to the recorder's hut. This is a place of sanctuary, in a way, for players. It is where the numbers are totted up and the card is signed, which is every bit as important as any drive or pitch or putt.

Once he had signed his card, Harrington turned to the television and watched as García came up the 18th fairway. He watched as García played his bunker shot from a greenside trap. He watched as García pulled his belly-putter into his midriff and stroked the ball towards the hole. He watched as it refused to drop. In that moment his mood changed. He put his game face back on.

As one, Harrington and Flood got up and left to spend a few moments on the putting green where the time spent was as much about talking with Rotella as the need to hole putts. After all, Harrington's 67 to García's 73 in the final round reaffirmed his belief — despite the shenanigans on the last hole — that he, not his rival, had played the best golf. But the play-off, with aggregate scores over four holes, was a fresh start. They were starting from scratch.

The play-off to find a player to follow in the footsteps of previous winners at Carnoustie — Tommy Armour in 1931, Henry Cotton in 37, Ben Hogan in 53, Gary Player in 68, Tom Watson in 72 and Paul Lawrie in 99 — involved a four-hole battle over the first, 16th, 17th and 18th holes. There could be only one winner.

The first hole, a par 4 of 406 yards, is known to this day as Cup. As Woods had discovered in his second round when hooking an iron into the burn, it could be tougher than it looked. In winning the Claret Jug in 53, Hogan hit a two-iron approach. Technology had progressed hugely and, when Harrington's five-wood landed in the middle of the fairway, he was left with nothing more than a seven-iron for his approach.

García hit first and found a semi-plugged lie in a greenside bunker. Harrington's approach shaped his destiny: it finished 10 feet from the pin and, importantly, was on the same line as the one he'd missed for birdie when he'd started out some five hours earlier. This time there was no mistake. He rolled in the birdie, and García missed his par save. A birdie to a bogey, Harrington had grabbed the initiative from the get-go.

The next hole was the par 3 16th, known as Barry Burn. Harrington missed the green with his rescue club and finished in a swale. García's body language after his tee shot hit the flagstick and spun away to 18 feet told the story of a man who believed the golfing gods were against him. Harrington got up and down for his par, and García two-putted for his. The two-shot advantage remained with Harrington.

Pars from each of them on the 17th meant Harrington returned to the scene of the crime — the 18th tee — with a two-shot lead. It wasn't a time for heroics. In his mind, he decided to play it as a par 5. He found the fairway off the tee with his favoured utility club, laid up short of the burn, and from there hit his approach to 30 feet. Two putts later, for bogey, and Harrington raised his putter to the skies as the Champion Golfer of 2007.

The presentation ceremony was special, not just for the fact that Pádraig Harrington had ended a 60-year drought since Fred Daly's Open win of 1947. Another Irish golfer was also part of the celebration. Rory McIlroy won the Silver Medal as leading amateur and had announced himself to the golfing world. But this was Harrington's time, Harrington's moment. A certain Mr Faldo had got his answer about the new generation.

But it was his son Paddy who kept him on planet earth. For much of the summer, father and son had spent any spare time searching for ladybirds in the garden of their home in the foothills of the Dublin mountains. 'Can we put ladybirds in it?' wondered Paddy as he looked at the most famous trophy in the golfing world. 'We can indeed. We can indeed,' replied his father, the champion.

The first drink out of the Claret Jug under Pádraig Harrington's watch was John Smith's ale.

The golfer himself only rarely drank, and the ale wouldn't have been his drink of choice on any other occasion, but Harrington — more often seen with a Diet Coke in his hand — had promised his manager Adrian Mitchel, his long-time handler at IMG, that John Smith's rather than claret or any other beverage would be the first celebratory drink out of the Jug.

Harrington and his entourage celebrated his breakthrough Major win with a shindig in the IMG house that went on until four o'clock in the morning. By six, he was awake again.

On the morning after his triumph, Harrington recalled his sleepless first night as Open champion. 'I was wide awake (at six). I woke up my wife and said, I'm the Open champion. The trophy was at the end of the bed and both of us are looking at it. Then she said, "I can't believe it. There's the trophy . . . but can we go back to sleep?" Caroline is like myself. A lot of those around me who've been supporting me over the years believed I'd win it more than I have myself. I've always had all the support in the world from Caroline, but I think we're still in disbelief.'

As the wind coming off the North Sea rattled the R&A media tent on that Monday morning, Harrington paid special tribute to his septuagenarian coach Bob Torrance, a Scot who worked with his eyes and feel rather than computer software. 'I'm thrilled for Bob. He is such a part of this. He has worked tirelessly on my game and never stops thinking about it. For me to go out and win a Major is very special for Bob. And for me to win a Major at Carnoustie, because Bob loves (Ben) Hogan so much, is the icing on the cake.'

Hogan had won the 1953 Open championship at Carnoustie and had served as an inspiration to Harrington as he worked on his own game. As Harrington put it: 'The guys I have always admired as my idols have not necessarily been unbelievably talented. I have more admired the guys who have worked hard on the game and got the most out of their talent. Hogan went from being a struggling professional to probably the best ball-striker of all time and definitely one of the best golfers of all time. He is definitely someone I would hold up as a role model. Originally, I would have thought of Hogan in terms of just pure hard work, but there was a lot more behind the man and a lot of his mental skills were very strong . . . The more I hear about him, the more I like and admire him.'

And, on that morning, Harrington set his sights on winning again . . . and again.

'When Phil Mickelson was asked if he was ever going to win a Major, he said: "I'm going to win more than one Major." That's the importance of having a goal. If it does happen that you win a Major, if it was your only and sole goal, if that's the ultimate of your goals, it's not far off the finish of your career. You always have to have goals to keep moving forward, so I've always had it in my head to try and win more than one Major. So that should help me to move on from this championship. If my goal was to win one Major, you'd have a situation it would be hard to move on from, but I'll definitely try to win more.'

Chapter 4 ∿

BEWARE THE INJURED GOLFER . . .

137th Open Championship, Royal Birkdale
Golf Club, Lancashire, England

July 2008

Saturday 12 July

The scene is the gym in Pádraig Harrington's plush family home in Rathmichael, south County Dublin. In truth, it is more than a gym. It is an indoor golfing academy with head-high mirrors, all sorts of gadgets and enough room to swing a dozen cats, never mind a single golf club.

But that is what the 2007 Open champion is doing. He is repeatedly hitting a driver into an impact bag as part of an exercise designed to strengthen a player's wrist. Henry Cotton used to do it, except he used old car tyres. Harrington's focus was an up-to-date impact bag. Same idea, though.

It is an exercise he has been doing for years without any problems.

Problems? Never say never. There is always a first time. For everything.

What makes Harrington's work-out all the more surprising is not the late hour — he is known to work on his swing or under

floodlights on the holes he built in his garden until his wife Caroline
begs him to call time — but the fact that, just a few hours previously,
the Dubliner had retained his Irish PGA *Championship title at the*
European Club in Co. Wicklow, which made his desire to continue
working a little strange. His game was good. His confidence was
good. He was on course. He was ticking all the boxes.

But here he was. In the downstairs area of his house. Hitting a
bean bag.

Whoooossssh!

The driver is driven into the bag.

Whoooossssh!

120 miles per hour.

Time.

Whoooossssh!

And time again.

Whoooossssh!

Then, he lets out a cry. Of pain. Real pain.

Harrington, five days before he is due to commence the defence of
his Open Championship title at Royal Birkdale on the Lancashire
coast, has damaged his right wrist.

Immediately, he knew he was in trouble.

———

On the Sunday, the day after sustaining his wrist injury,
Harrington travelled across the Irish Sea wondering if he would
be able to actually defend the title he had won in a dramatic
fashion at Carnoustie twelve months previously. But his first port

of call was not Royal Birkdale. Instead, he made his way to Hesketh Golf Club where the R&A's Junior Open was taking place with more than a hundred competitors from some 70 countries.

It said a lot about Harrington as a person that he fulfilled the appointment. He couldn't hold a club. He couldn't sign an autograph. But he could talk. And he did, to young players from around the globe who looked up to him as a champion golfer.

He didn't let them down.

But would he let himself down? 'If it wasn't the Open I wouldn't be here. I'd have pulled out on Sunday. It is definitely an injury that you wouldn't risk,' said Harrington, who genuinely wondered if he would be able to play in the actual championship.

For sure, it curtailed his preparations. If it weren't so serious, it would have been funny. Not Billy Connolly funny, more M-A-S-H ha-ha. Just a month earlier, Tiger Woods had won the US Open at Torrey Pines on one leg. Harrington's wrist meant he was setting out to defend his Open title with one good hand. Nobody was laughing.

Dale Richardson, an Australian physical therapist and an integral part of Harrington's team, had been notified by phone of his man's injury. It was Sunday. Richardson was actually in Scotland at the Barclays Scottish Open — where Graeme McDowell fine-tuned his game for Birkdale with an impressive win — and couldn't assess the extent of the injury until player and medical man met up.

The diagnosis? It was, as Richardson put it after finally getting to his man in Birkdale, 'a first degree strain of the pronator quadratus . . . and there's also a problem with his flexor. It's a strained wrist of the soft tissues in some of the soft muscles that stabilise the wrist.' The medical speak sounded impressive, but it was Harrington's lack of preparation in the run-up to his championship defence that alerted everyone to the seriousness of the injury.

In the days before any tournament, Harrington — like every other player in the field — would get in a number of practice rounds to gauge how and what way a course was playing. In that week, the Dubliner managed a grand total of nine holes before he was called to the first tee on Thursday as the defending champion.

On Tuesday, Harrington officially returned the Claret Jug to the R&A. His year as its custodian had finished, although — even with the injury that was lingering and niggling his every thought — he found time to show some humour. He asked the R&A if it would be possible to get a smaller box so that he could bring the trophy with him more readily on planes.

Harrington limited himself to playing just nine holes of practice on the Tuesday of Open week, with strict instructions from Richardson that he was not to hit any shots out of the rough. After playing the front nine alongside Damien McGrane and Woody Austin, the golfer sought out Richardson and found that the wrist, as anticipated, had weakened. He rejoined his playing partners but limited himself to an occasional chip and putt. Otherwise, his time was spent walking the back nine on a familiarisation exercise.

'It's amazing. Sometimes when you deal with Dale, he is very blasé about it. Dale's quite happy he can get a job done on it so long as I don't overdo it. I'll definitely be teeing up . . . Probably the biggest worry is if I hit it in the rough during the tournament and risk doing something to it and it flares up again. It's inflamed, like a sprain, and I'll probably strap it up during the tournament.'

Harrington's daily medical report dominated the run-up to the championship at Royal Birkdale, one which had lost the world No. 1 Tiger Woods who underwent knee surgery after his play-off win over Rocco Mediate in the US Open.

———

In the absence of Woods, Phil Mickelson was left to answer as many questions about Woods as about his own game. Mickelson, who kindly allowed Harrington the use of a medical device to alleviate the wrist sprain, refused to accept the bait from his inquisitors, as he deflected any reference to Tiger's absence and batted it away with the ease of a baseball player at the plate.

Question: 'No Tiger here. People are saying that the Majors are being devalued. What's your thought on this? Do you think that it is a slight on the rest of the profession? Or is there an element of truth in it?'

Mickelson: 'I am working hard to get my game ready for this week and I've practised hard. I've developed a good game plan for this event, and I am excited to compete against whoever is in the field.'

Question: 'I mean, you can't say anything in particular about Tiger?

Mickelson: 'Oh, I'm sure I could . . . but right now my focus is, again, this week. I've got my game sharp . . . Right now it's short game for me and getting my chipping and putting strong.'

In other words, don't mention TW. He wasn't there. He couldn't win.

Yet, one man, Geoff Ogilvy, one of the most cerebral players on tour, didn't mind tackling the Woods issue head on. 'I just hope they've taught the engraver how to put an asterisk on the trophy, then everyone will know what the tournament was all about,' he joked. 'No, if any tournament can stand up strong when he (Woods) is not around, it is this one and the US Open and the Masters and the (US) PGA. I mean, the events are bigger than any one guy. Tiger obviously adds to any tournament you play, but the Open is the Open.'

Point made.

———

Whilst Mickelson and Ogilvy were left to deal with the absence of Woods from the championship, Harrington — the defending champion — still had a lot to occupy his mind as he headed out to the course on the eve of the tournament. On Wednesday, most players will limit their play to nine holes. A few will play 18. Others might decide to spend the majority of their time around the short game area and on the range. Different strokes for different folks, in effect.

Harrington — with just nine holes of preparation — was anxious to test out his wrist. It didn't work out too well. He hit a total of three shots (two off the tee, one from the middle of the fairway) before a jarring pain brought his pre-championship work to a premature end. He put his chances of being able to play in the championship at 'no more than 75 per cent'.

On his return to the course, Harrington became a keen observer of how others played the course. He watched Doug

McGuigan, Hennie Otto, Jeff Overton and Darren Fichardt. He watched, and he absorbed. He was a good learner.

His preparation had been far from ideal, but Harrington ruled out taking any cortisone injection to improve his chances of playing. He sought to take a philosophical approach. 'I'm not in control of the wrist injury. It is not something I can worry about. If I was playing badly or putting badly or something like that, I would be worried because I would be trying to fix it. But somebody else is trying to fix my wrist, so that's why I am not too stressed.'

——

As if Royal Birkdale wasn't a tough enough layout, the first day of the 137th Open Championship on Thursday brought some wicked weather and winds that reached 30 miles an hour.

But Pádraig Harrington's wrist survived all that the course and the weather could throw at it. His alarm clock had sounded at 4.55 am and a quick look outside the bedroom window revealed murky clouds that would combine with strong winds. He knew the opening round of his defence of the Claret Jug would be a battle — just the way he liked it.

The good news was that, finally, the wrist injury which had severely disrupted his preparation had responded to Dale Richardson's treatment. Harrington opened his account with a 74, which left him five strokes behind first round leaders Graeme McDowell — a week on from his Scottish Open win — Robert Allenby and Rocco Mediate.

Harrington stayed away from any post-round work on the range for fear of aggravating the right wrist. 'At one stage of my career,' he said, 'you'd probably see me head back out to the range on a day like this. But I've matured a little. I wouldn't go because of the injury but, injury or not, no. I realise that you aren't going to find anything out there (in the conditions).'

Harrington had got out of his bed that morning not knowing if he could swing a club. He got to the range at 7 am and started a warm-up routine that saw him gradually build up from sand wedge to fairway woods to the driver. Watched closely by Bob Torrance, he felt what he termed only 'three or four' twinges that were 'bearable'. By the time he teed off at 7.58 am, he knew in his heart he could survive a round.

'I was apprehensive about hitting out of the rough, but when it didn't hurt on the first, I got more relaxed . . . I think the tougher weather helped because, as bad as it was, you could only focus on your next shot and on getting your grip dry. There was very little time to be distracted, and that was good for my wrist. It's a respectable enough score. I've to focus on the positive, that there are 54 holes, (and) that my wrist should be getting better and better.'

Ah, such foresight!

On that day, though, McDowell was the happiest Irishman. G-Mac, as he's known to friend and foe alike, had benefited from a later tee time. The wind persisted but the rain had stopped, and McDowell acknowledged: 'I was happy. I plodded my way around. The guys (in the morning) looked like they had a really, really tough time in the wind and rain. We just had the wind to deal with. It was blowing hard, but you can always handle one or the other, wind or rain, but together it's a pretty tough combo.'

McDowell had led the first round of the Open at Hoylake in 2006, only to go into reverse when it really mattered. 'I felt like a rabbit caught in the headlights (in 2006),' recalled the Ulsterman of that experience. 'I was like, what's this all about? Now, I feel like a different player than I was two years ago when I didn't have a whole lot of belief in my game. It caught up with me on the weekend, and Tiger (Woods) left the field in his dust.'

He added: 'Links short game is a completely different fish from the short game we're faced with week in and week out . . . It requires imagination, and playing golf in the wind requires flight control. It is all about shaping the ball against the wind, under-standing how the wind affects the ball. I'm not the best shaper of a ball, but I've got a pretty good understanding of how the wind affects shots and getting in my head what a certain flight is going to do.'

There were a lot of great shots hit that day, and a lot of poor ones. Phil Mickelson was one of those who struggled. On the sixth hole he hooked his second shot into the dunes and his ball was not found. He signed for a 79. The biggest role he would play in the week was allowing Harrington to visit his hotel to avail of the medical device to alleviate his wrist injury!

But there were surprises too, and on that opening day one of them was delivered by Greg Norman. In his heyday, which included lengthy spells as the world's No. 1 ranked golfer, Norman — who was given the moniker, the 'Great White Shark', because of his looks, flowing blond hair and his fierce competitive instincts — had reserved his very best performances for the Open. He was a winner in 1986 and again in 93.

He arrived at Royal Birkdale with no great expectations,

however. The Australian had recently married former tennis player Chris Evert, hadn't played in an Open championship since 2005 and made only rare forays out on to the competitive circuit. In fact, he'd played just three times on the US Tour that season and had missed the cut on each occasion: in the AT&T National Pro-Am at Pebble Beach, the Mayakoba tournament and the AT&T Classic.

Nobody was more surprised than Norman when he opened his campaign with a 70, just one stroke adrift of the leaders. 'I've got to keep my expectations realistically low, to be honest with you. I haven't played a lot of golf . . . it's just like riding a bike. But even riding a bike sometimes after a long time, you're a little wobbly. I've got to manage the process the best I can. I've just got to take one shot at a time and see what happens.'

The scores on the board at the end of a wicked first round told its own story: only three players had managed to break par; a further three had scored par; and 148 players were above the par of 70. Ernie Els and Vijay Singh both failed to break 80. It was that kind of tough day at the office, when many players were forced to lick their wounds and soothe damaged egos.

———

On Thursday evening, Graeme McDowell sat down to watch a DVD with those closest to him, his father Kenny, his mother Marian and his manager Conor Ridge. It was a feel-good reel. He knew the plot and knew how it would end. It was a DVD of his win in the previous Sunday's Scottish Open. It hinted of more glory in bigger events down the line.

On Friday, G-Mac followed up his opening 69 with a 73 that was chiselled out of difficult conditions. He had slipped from the lofty perch he occupied after day one, but he remained firmly in the thick of the hunt. 'I had a slow start,' he observed. 'You know, four or five days of swinging the golf club in this kind of wind inevitably takes its toll. I felt my rhythm wasn't quite there for the first 10 or 11 holes.'

In fact, McDowell was four-over-par through 11 holes and finding it all a bit of a battle. 'I was still looking at it that the glass was half-full,' he said of the mindset that rescued his round, as he covered the last seven holes in one-under.

If McDowell was daring to dream of what it would be like to clasp the Claret Jug close to his chest, so too were others. KJ Choi, for one. The son of a Korean rice farmer, Choi had never lifted a golf club until his mid-teens at the behest of his school's athletics coach. It proved to be the best piece of school guidance he ever got as he carved out a hugely successful career on the fairways of the world.

Choi shot a second round 67 to assume the midway lead on 139 — one-under-par — but the romantics were more concerned with the second coming of the Great White Shark than with the son of the rice farmer.

Norman shot a second successive round of 70 that left him all alone in second place. As the novelist H. G. Wells had put it: 'I want to go ahead of Father Time with a scythe of my own.' It seemed that Norman, a sprightly recently divorced and then quickly newly-wed 53-year old, was doing just that; except, in his case the Aussie used the 14 clubs in his golf bag to fend off the demons of time.

In defying Father Time, Norman — a two-time Open champion but whose clubs had been gathering dust in recent years as he concentrated on entrepreneurial and global business activities — relived past glories that had people shaking their heads incredulously. It took another old-timer Tom Watson to point out that he had always considered Norman one of the game's best bad weather players ever.

'My expectations were almost nil coming in,' admitted the Aussie. 'Honestly, there's probably less pressure on me than anybody here because, even though I'm in the position I'm in, I'm going to go out there and just say, hey, just go have fun.'

Norman's unexpected challenge was just one of a number of compelling tales. What of David Duval's equally unexpected renaissance? The champion of 2001, Duval had found more solace in family life and in snowboarding than on the golf course after his win. At Birkdale, Duval was more like his old self as he shot a second round 69 to jump the septet of players bunched on 142, in tied-fourth.

There were other intriguing stories from that Friday. Camilo Villegas, for one. The Colombian reeled off five successive birdies from the 14th to gatecrash the party with a 65, two strokes off the best ever round in all of the Opens down the years at Birkdale.

And yet Harrington's tigerish tenacity was as meritorious as any other deeds. He had travelled across the Irish Sea by helicopter on the previous Sunday to attend the R&A Junior Open but unsure if he could actually defend his championship. He could barely lift a club, never mind swing one. But he managed to play and, not only that, he managed to contend. At one stage of his second round, it seemed as if the wheels had come off when he had back-to-back bogeys on the 10th and 11th holes. His response was to finish eagle-birdie at the 17th and 18th to post a 68 and join those on 142.

On the 11th, he had grimaced as he attempted to extricate a shot from heavy rough. 'It just gave me a bit of a fright that it hurt my wrist. That's why I let go of the club.' Although it didn't match the brilliance of Villegas's close-out, it came darn close.

The evidence of Harrington's true well-being came late, timed perfectly to bring that focused look from Carnoustie a year ago back to his facial features. The Irishman's run of birdie-par-eagle-birdie from the 15th revitalised his challenge.

The eagle came on the 17th, where a three-wood off the tee carried 282 yards and then bounded on a further 61 yards to leave him with 229 yards to the pin. Harrington's five-iron approach finished pin high, 30 feet away, and he rolled in the eagle putt to invigorate his challenge.

On the 18th, Harrington again used his three-wood off the tee and, slightly fortuitous to evade the fairway bunker on the elbow down the right, he made the most of his break with a superb nine-iron approach from 183 yards that nestled five feet behind the hole. He sank the birdie putt, and the bogey-bogey finish of the previous day had been forgotten. On those two holes he had made up five shots on his previous day's effort. His challenge for the Claret Jug was again very much alive.

Of his position three shots behind the leader, Harrington — who was six shots behind Sergio García at the same juncture the previous year — said: 'I'm delighted. I'm well in there with 36 holes to go . . . It's exactly where you want to be. It's unlikely any-body is going to run away with it because the conditions are meant to be tough, so I just want to make sure with nine holes to go I give myself a chance.'

The glint had returned to his eyes. A year on from Carnoustie, Harrington knew he was knocking on the door again.

———

There were, it seemed, a number of unlikely contenders as the third round of the 137th Open worked its way through a long, cold day. For many, it was a battle merely to survive. The winds gusted to as much as 50 miles per hour at times and there were many who were literally blown away. One of them was Graeme McDowell, who fell from contention with a horrendous 80 that saw him fall down the leaderboard much like a stone in a well. It was another lesson to put into the memory bank.

McDowell wasn't alone, of course. It was to be a day when not a single player broke par. Of the 83 players who made the cut, just four managed to match par. The other 79 shot scores above the par of 70. Nine of them — among them Justin Rose and David Duval who shot 83s — scored 80 or higher.

Birkdale showed absolutely no mercy.

Phil Mickelson's hat was blown clear off his head. Simon Wakefield, a tall and lean competitor, was himself blown over. Flag sticks were whipped out of tin cups. Camilo Villegas had played with wizardry and a sense of invincibility in compiling a 65 on Friday, but signed for a 79, 14 strokes worse off, after a bruising third round.

Forewarned by the weathermen about the wind's ferocity, the R&A had reacted by placing the pins on the flatter parts of the greens and even moved up the tee on three holes. Even so, there was a stage when it looked as if they would have to suspend play. There were reports of balls not only oscillating but actually moving considerable distances on the greens. American Anthony Kim, for one, saw his ball move 15 yards from its original position and off the green. Fortunately for him he had just marked it in time. Sweden's Fredrik Jacobson even had a ball move on him in a bunker.

In such circumstances, some players coped better than others. Wakefield may have been battered by the wind, but he kept more control than most and was one of four players to post a round of 70. It enabled him to leapfrog from 22nd position at the start of the day up to fourth. Ben Curtis, the 2003 champion, also shot a 70 to move from 38th to fifth and into contention.

The magic of the Open, however, was epitomised by the man who finished the day as the outright leader. Greg Norman had four bogeys in his opening 10 holes and looked to be in danger of returning to the pack, only to rediscover some of his old creative magic on the run for home. The Aussie covered the final eight holes in two-under-par — six pars and two birdies, on the 14th and 17th — and signed for a 72 for a 54-hole total of 212, two-over-par. It gave him a two-shot lead over defending champion Pádraig Harrington and KJ Choi.

Choi had one of the game's most experienced caddies on his bag. Andy Prodger, an Englishman who won two Majors with Nick Faldo (the 1987 Open and the 89 Masters), had formed an unlikely partnership with the Korean. 'Andy is like my big brother. He's like an uncle at times. He just makes me feel very relaxed and comfortable. We make a good team,' explained Choi, who managed to record a 75 for 214.

On that day Choi got a close-up and personal view of Norman's ability to get the ball into the hole. 'He is a very imaginative player, more imaginative than me,' he conceded.

Norman's shot-making was all about feel. The yardage book was effectively put aside as he used an array of shots to negotiate his way around. On the fifth hole, with only 120 yards to the flag, he punched a five-iron. On the 17th, with 209 yards to the pin, he hit a six-iron and sent the ball out over the grandstand and allowed the wind to bring it back. It was a display of links golf at its purest. 'I've played under tougher weather conditions, but in the third round of a Major championship on the Royal Birkdale course, it was just brutal,' conceded the Shark.

Of all the players in the field, Harrington — who had prepared for the championship in exactly the same fashion as the previous year when playing in and winning the Irish PGA at the European — was the one most capable of living with the conditions. In his mind, a significant percentage of the field were inclined to concede defeat too readily when the weather conditions were bad. His approach was to keep the head down, play one shot at a time and stay focused. 'You're probably looking at close to 40 per cent of the field that really aren't prepared to play in weather like that. So it gives you a big advantage.'

It wasn't all plain sailing, of course, for Harrington in the third round. Far from it, in fact. He three-putted the 11th green for bogey and his tee shot on the short 12th caught a gust of wind that flung the ball into heavy rough on a sand-hill. It resulted in a double-bogey five. He refused to be unnerved and grabbed birdies at the 15th and 17th that combined with an up-and-down par save on the 18th to leave a satisfied smile on his face.

Harrington's smile was only the third widest of the evening. The widest belonged to Norman and his new wife Chris Evert. Only a month previously they had been on honeymoon in the Bahamas. Now, at the age of 53, he was leading the Open. 'I think it's a great indicator for every player out there, whether you're just coming on the tour for the first year or you're turning 40 or in your 50s. The game of golf is there to be played. If you go in with the right attitude and keep yourself physically fit, you can put yourself in that position no matter what.'

Although only ranked 646th in the world ahead of the championship, Norman had used all his experience and creativity — along with a relaxed mindset of limited expectations — to get into position. Harrington, for one, wasn't surprised. The two had become friends when Norman designed the wonderful Doonbeg links in Co. Clare, and had even faced each other in a match to officially open the course on huge sand dunes overlooking the Atlantic. 'He is as fit a 53-year old as there is, and when he puts his mind to it, he can certainly play. He hasn't lost any of his ability.'

Neither had Harrington.

Although he had failed to win on the PGA European Tour or the US PGA Tour since his triumph at Carnoustie, Harrington still knew how to finish a deal. Years of toiling on courses around the globe, notching up wins in places as far removed as South America and Asia as well as the powerhouses of Europe and the United States had chiselled the rough diamond who left the amateur ranks in 1995 into one of professional golf's true gems.

———

There is an old adage in the game of golf. It is, 'Beware the injured golfer.' And there have been numerous instances of players defying injury — or perhaps using it as a distraction so that their mind is entirely focused on the job at hand — to go out and win Major championships.

Just a month previously Tiger Woods had won the US Open at Torrey Pines outside San Diego in California despite being in such discomfort with a knee ailment that he had barely hoisted the trophy aloft when he announced he was taking a break to undergo surgery. What's more, Woods had to go to a full 18-hole play-off to account for Rocco Mediate.

There was no Woods at Royal Birkdale. But that didn't lessen the drama or take away from one of the greatest story lines of any Open. After all, Norman provided the romance of a man past his prime returning to his favourite Major of all to fight tooth and nail for another Claret Jug.

And then there was Harrington — defending — who had arrived at the event nursing a wrist injury and unsure if he would be able to hold a club let alone swing it.

Only those chosen by destiny hear the call. Only the truly great ones hear it twice. Harrington, a policeman's son from the foothills of the Dublin mountains, clearly heard the call and was drawn to it. Unlike the previous year when he triumphed at Carnoustie, his repeat victory — emulating the feats of Tiger Woods, Tom Watson, Lee Trevino and Arnold Palmer who had all successfully defended in their time — didn't have any heart-stopping moments. There was no Barry Burn to suck the ball into its chill waters. There was no need for any play-off.

Harrington won the oldest major of them all with a command

performance that smacked of true greatness. A final round 69 for 283, three-over-par, gave Harrington a four-stroke winning margin over England's Ian Poulter, while Greg Norman — who had started the day with a two-shot lead — finished in a tie for third place with Sweden's Henrik Stenson. In retaining the trophy, the most prized in golf, Harrington became the first European player to do so since James Braid performed the feat in 1906. He also became the first European player ever to win the Open at Birkdale.

Unlike Carnoustie, when Harrington got a jump start on the final couple of groups and posted his score, this time he had to wait until the final tee time — 2.20 pm — where he was introduced on the tee alongside Norman by the official announcer Ivor Robson. Norman, a real blast from the past, was greeted by a huge roar as he walked on to the tee box. But the one that met Harrington was every bit as loud, if not more so. They loved their golf on the Lancashire coast and a large number of Harrington's supporters had made the short trip across the Irish Sea to cheer on their man.

As the wind whipped in off the Irish Sea and over the sand-hills, Norman's two-shot advantage had disappeared by the time the Irishman and the Australian made it to the third tee box. By the time the pair walked off the third green, where Harrington made a fine sand save, the pendulum had swung firmly in the direction of the defending champion. Norman endured a nightmare start to his outrageous if romantic bid to win the Claret Jug at the age of 53. He started bogey-bogey-bogey and, within an hour of his final round, had slipped from leader to chaser.

It got no better for Norman on the par 4 sixth hole, which had ranked as the toughest of all on the previous three days. Norman played army golf. He drove into the rough down the left of the fairway and then found the right rough with his attempted recovery. Left. Right. It led to another bogey, and as the galleries groaned in sympathy, Harrington moved into a two-shot lead.

Golf, especially in the final round of a Major, is prone to ask stern questions. Harrington was not immune from such challenges and endured a leaky period of his own mid-round as he suffered three successive bogeys from the seventh to the ninth holes. Indeed, the Irishman got a fortunate break on the ninth where his approach missed the green and finished a matter of inches from gorse bushes. He bogeyed it, but it could have been much worse. It was to be Harrington's last dropped shot of his final round.

The roars from ahead indicated to Harrington that someone was making a charge. That man was Ian Poulter. When Poulter birdied the 16th hole — which moved him to seven-over-par — he was at that point in a three-way tie for the lead with Harrington and Norman, who had steadied matters considerably after his shaky start. But Poulter, who had missed a glorious birdie opportunity on the par 5 15th, then failed to birdie the par 5 17th.

As the home crowds gave added vocal encouragement to Poulter's charge, Harrington re-energised his own quest for another Open title. On the 13th, Harrington hit a five-iron approach to 15 feet and sank the putt for the first birdie of his round. Then on the 544-yard par 5 15th, Harrington found the green in two and two-putted from distance for a birdie that moved him two strokes clear of Poulter and three ahead of Norman.

Poulter had finished his round, signed his card and moved on to the practice ground in anticipation of a possible play-off. But

Harrington's birdies on the 13th and 15th had given him a sniff of victory in his nostrils. He was on a march of his own.

As he moved closer to home, Harrington seemed to get better and better. The best of all came on the par 5 17th hole. After a good tee shot with his five-wood, his favourite club, Harrington was left with 249 yards to the pin. He reached again for the five-wood and smashed the ball towards the green where it conveniently bounced over a greenside bunker, took the contours of the bumpy green and ran up to three feet from the cup. It was an approach shot worthy of a champion and effectively closed the deal for the Irishman.

Unlike the previous year, when he twice walked down the 18th fairway at Carnoustie with enormous pressure on his shoulders and unable to savour the acclaim of the galleries, his walk down the final fairway at Birkdale was stress free. He used a three-wood off the tee, which took the out-of-bounds down the right out of play, found the fairway and then, with his adrenalin flowing, hit a five-iron approach of 194 yards through the crosswind to the green. Two putts later he was in possession of the Claret Jug for another 12 months.

'I hit the ball as pure as I could, and just felt really good,' said Harrington. 'I felt comfortable, really played within myself . . . I was just trying to convince myself it would be my day. I didn't get ahead of myself at any stage.'

In fact, Harrington avoided looking at any scoreboards. 'I have a wandering mind at times and I struggle when I get into the lead. That's why I don't watch leaderboards. I struggle when I relax. I need a little tension, something to keep me focused . . . and there's no question the weather, the wind, forced me to play one shot at a time and stay with my own game.'

Norman was gracious in defeat. 'The way he finished, a true champion finishes that way,' he opined. Nobody argued.

―――

When Pádraig Harrington sank the winning putt in the play-off with Sergio García at Carnoustie, his son Paddy had found a use for the famous Claret Jug. After his win at Royal Birkdale, Harrington forecast a different use of the trophy. 'My son has gone a little past ladybirds at this stage. I think he is more into snails and more gruesome insects now.'

The embrace by the 18th green from his wife Caroline and Paddy was every bit as emotional as the year previously in Carnoustie. But there was one difference: there was another Harrington in the group hug. Their youngest son, Ciarán, who had been born eight months previously, was on hand to witness his dad's triumph.

'Winning a major puts you into a special club. Winning two of them puts you into a new club altogether. I'm going to make sure I enjoy the next week . . . I've got a wrist injury, so I can't go and practise, so I'm okay for the week (to let the achievement sink in),' said Harrington.

―――

The successful defence of his title was remarkable for a number of reasons, but especially because Harrington had barely been able to hold a club in the days that led up to the tournament. He had been limited to just nine holes of practice and had undergone intensive treatment from his sports therapist Dale Richardson.

As he held the Claret Jug, shinier than when he had returned it to the R&A and with his name engraved for a second time, Harrington claimed that the disrupted build-up had actually worked to his benefit. Due to very strong winds throughout the four days, the Birkdale course proved to be one of the toughest championship examinations in many years. 'The wrist injury was a great distraction for me . . . There's no question it pushed everything about coming back to defend (the title) to the side. It took a lot of pressure off me. It took away a lot of stress. It was a good distraction to have.'

Indeed, there was another consequence. Aside from ensuring that he didn't think too much about the actual defence, the injury also kept him physically and mentally sharp. 'Everybody will tell you this has been the toughest week we could ever have in golf. The fact that I didn't play three practice rounds like normal for a major was a big bonus. I was very fresh going into the weekend. The wrist injury was a saver for me really.'

He added: 'The injury took all the pressure and stress and expectation away from my game. I think my case is slightly different to Tiger's. He was obviously injured throughout the tournament (the US Open at Torrey Pines) and it was impairing his ability to perform. My injury didn't impair me at all on the golf course. It kept me away from practice, which as it turned out was a bonus. Golfers are very fickle. Little things can change our mindset and our moods, and that can have a huge effect on our golf. Having a little bit of pressure release in terms of having a wrist injury was just what I needed to go out and play my own golf, to do my own thing and not try too hard.'

Although it was Harrington's first win on either the European Tour or the US Tour since his triumph at Carnoustie, he reiterated his stance that all of his preparations were geared to the Majors. 'My goal is to keep getting into contention in the Majors, to keep hanging around. The Majors are what it is all about for me. I set my schedule out this year for the four Majors and the Ryder Cup and I try to peak for those four weeks . . . If I can get a 50 per cent hit rate and get into contention, then that's two a year (to contend in). All you need to do is maybe hit one out of four of those and you're winning one every second year. That's a pretty high rate for most of us mere mortals.'

Harrington had joined an elite band of back-to-back champions in the Open with his success in Birkdale. How did he explain the transformation? 'It is about averages. Get yourself in position enough times and it will fall on the right side for you some of the time and the wrong side other times. But the key is to continue to get into position. I have seen it over the years where I have played great in tournaments and through no fault of my own I have finished second. And I have seen where I messed up and finished second. And over those tournaments I have had to sit there and try and make some sense of it. I had a lot of long chats with just about everybody, Bob Rotella, my brother Tadhg, discussing the merits of why me, why didn't I win this tournament? We eventually came to the conclusion that it is just a question of averages and keeping yourself in those positions. One day you will hole that 10 footer on the last to get into the play-off, and the next day it doesn't go in and you lose the tournament. You can't control everything in golf and that is probably the key thing. You can get yourself into position, but you can't control all the breaks.

'On other days you will fight as hard as you can and it just won't happen. I thought Greg Norman played well and it just didn't happen for him. It drifted away from him. He got a terrible start without doing anything wrong and the momentum was all with me. A chip and putt on the first and that kicked me off. You just don't know how much that affects the rest of the day. It is all about averages.'

Harrington, though, had proven he was far from your average golfer. He was a multi-Major champion.

THE KEY SHOT

Five-wood approach to the 17th to set up an eagle

'I'd got 220 yards to the front (of the green), 249 to the pin. My caddie (Ronan Flood) said to me, "You know, if you want to think of laying up . . ." I asked him the situation. He said, "You're two ahead." I just felt I knew I could make birdie if I hit five-wood. I knew that was going to make me (the champion). I was anxious that Greg (Norman) could make eagle going down there and if I made lay-up and I make par, all of a sudden I've got a one-shot lead . . . I wasn't so much worried about the guy who was two shots behind me and finished, being Ian Poulter. It was more I was worried if I laid up and made par I was giving Greg a great chance to get within one shot of me, and one shot is not comfortable in any shape or form going down 18.

'So I wanted to take it on. The downslope I convinced myself, as you can when you're winning tournaments, was a help to me. My ball was on quite a hanging lie and I thought, this is great, it is going to come out low so I can't get it in the air. The only thing I knew was a problem was if I put the ball up in the air for a long time. It could obviously find its way into the trouble on the right, or I could maybe get it into trouble on the left. But a low shot, I felt, was always going to be an advantage. So the downslope, I used it in my favour. It came out nice and low. Once I hit it, it was perfect. It's one of the few times I think I've ever heard my caddie say good shot before the ball is finished ... It was a real bonus, obviously, to finish three feet away. You know, you can't have enough shots in the lead going down 18. I proved that last year. So I was making sure to hole that (eagle putt) and take my four-shot lead, and it helped me enjoy the last hole.'

Chapter 5 ∿

MOVING TO AN IRISH RHYTHM IN MOTOWN . . .

90th PGA Championship, Oakland Hills,
Detroit, Michigan, USA

August 2008

Monday morning, 11 August
The day after madness descended.
Pádraig Harrington sits on a poolside deck-chair in a rented house
on a leafy street called Indian Mound West. It's in the township of
Bloomfield on the good side of Detroit and far removed from the
world of 8 Mile and Eminem's rap words. Two Pinkerton security
men have arrived to collect the Wanamaker trophy which just
happens to be perched on a drinks table beside an even older Major
trophy, the Claret Jug. The water on the surface of the swimming
pool glistens. The sun sparkles off the two silver trophies. It matches
the glint in the golfer's eyes.

Harrington, a policeman's son from south Dublin, is sitting with
a grin as wide as Dublin Bay.

His nine-month-old son Ciarán is sitting on his knees. The son's
facial expression is different from his father's. He is wondering what
these strange men with Dictaphones and smiles to equal his dad's are
doing in the garden that has been his playground for a week. He's

wondering why the Pinkerton men in their shiny uniforms are hovering with intent, eager to take the huge silver trophy from his daddy and put it into their van. For safe-keeping.

The son's eyes search for his mother Caroline and for older brother Paddy. He sees his grandmother Breda standing by the rear door.

Harrington, the father, is the picture of contentment. He is in shorts with a Hollister t-shirt.

Happy days!

The proud dad is talking about how, the day before, he has won his third Major and second Major in succession of a career that has exploded into space like a rocket. He is talking about how he is in a new stratosphere. He is looking back to less than 24 hours previously, when his eyes took on a manic, obsessive stare as he chased down other pretenders to the US PGA Championship on the South Course at Oakland Hills Country Club.

'You know,' he says, 'when I get those scary eyes, I do things.'

———

Those scary eyes were missing in Akron, Ohio, a week earlier. On the Sunday of the final round of the WGC-Bridgestone Invitational at Firestone Country Club, Harrington — two weeks to the day since he had defended the Claret Jug at Royal Birkdale — tapped in a putt for par to sign for a 67. It wasn't for a victory, but it was a gentle landing back to earth after the mayhem of his second Open championship win. The round confirmed to him that all was well with his game as he prepared to make the four hour road trip from Akron to Detroit for the next destination in a journey of Major venues that had taken on a life of its own. Oakland Hills Country Club beckoned.

Before he left Akron, it was mandatory to ask Harrington how he was. Any aches? Any pains? Injuries? Any ailments whatsoever? When he won his first British Open, the Irishman suffered from a crocked neck. When he defended the title, his wrist had been more than a bit troublesome. 'I always have something niggling, but at the moment nothing is constraining me playing. Let's say . . . I wouldn't like the PGA to be starting tomorrow, but I feel, over the next three days, I've a few things to tinker around with and I am hopeful to be ready by Thursday. I'd say I am where I expected to be.'

The drive from Akron to Detroit is as boring as they come, until you cross the Ohio-Michigan State border and land in the city where the car is king and its inhabitants hanker after the days when the sounds of Motown gave some sanity to a crazy world. Harrington arrived into town along with the other 155 players for the 90th PGA Championship with the reputation as golf's new-found 'Celtic Tiger'. He was a poster boy for Ireland, vibrant and successful. He mirrored the country's new image.

In the absence of Tiger Woods, who was rehabilitating from knee surgery, Harrington was the second ranked player in the world competing in the PGA. Only Phil Mickelson was ranked higher. As such, the two-time Open champion arrived with a greater sense of expectation — from others — than at any time in his career.

What's more, he knew the course. When the 2004 Ryder Cup match was held at Oakland Hills, Harrington had forged a successful partnership with his good friend Paul McGinley. The two Dubliners had been serenaded to the sound of 'Molly Malone' at one point, after teaming up to inflict a 4 & 3 defeat on Woods and Davis Love III in the second day's afternoon foursomes.

Of all the Ryder Cups in which Harrington played, that match was his best. He delivered, delivered big time. When it was all over and Bernhard Langer's Europe team had recorded an 18½ to 9½ win, Harrington — with four points from a possible five — walked away with good memories. Those good memories he was bringing back to the course just shy of four years later. He was a better player too. And a two-time Major winner to boot.

That Ryder Cup was remembered as much for the US captain Hal Sutton's decision to pair the world's top two players, Woods and Mickelson, together as it was for Europe's emphatic victory. Sutton believed, wrongly as it transpired, that the Woods-Mickelson partnership would be invincible.

Of his decision to pair them, Sutton observed: 'I told these two guys that I felt like the perception of the world was that the US team didn't bond and we didn't come together as a team. I don't know that we could pair two guys together that were more matched for one another than those two.'

Sutton's decision backfired in spectacular fashion. Colin Montgomerie, the talismanic figure of the European team, who seemed to grow in stature whenever the Ryder Cup came around, was paired with Harrington against the two American superstars in the first match of the competition.

Whilst Monty and Harrington seemed like blood brothers, the body language of Woods and Mickelson was entirely different. They stood over 10 yards apart from each other on the first tee. When it came to hitting their tee shots, it was akin to what is called 'army golf' of the left-right variety: Woods smashed his drive right; Mickelson curled his left into the scrubs. The Scotsman and the Irishman finished the match on the 17th green.

If everyone thought that Sutton had learnt his lesson, he hadn't. For the afternoon foursomes, the US captain again paired his two big guns together. Again they fired blanks. Pitched against Darren Clarke and Lee Westwood, Woods and Mickelson at least made it to the 18th tee all square with the Europeans, only to gift their opponents the match. Mickelson carved his drive out-of-bounds off the final tee, and the look on Woods's face left Sutton in no doubt about his poor decision-making in pairing them together. It was the last time Woods and Mickelson were partners in the Ryder Cup.

The course was one that had built up a ferocious reputation through the years. When the legendary Ben Hogan won the US Open championship in 1951, he remarked: 'I'm glad I brought this course, this monster, to its knees.' Designed by Donald Ross, the foremost golf course architect of his day, and opened for play in 1918, the South Course — followed some years later by the North Course — earned a reputation as a tough examination from early on. That Walter Hagen was installed as the club's professional only served to add to its lustre.

Over the years, the course — some 15 miles north-west of downtown Detroit — became one of the finest of any on the championship circuit. It played host to six US Opens and staged two US PGAS, won in 1972 by South African Gary Player and in 79 by Australian David Graham, before the season's final major returned in 2008 for a third visit. Its proximity to the Ryder Cup of 2004 seemed to give an extra pep to the Europeans, eager to end a drought in the Major known as 'Glory's Last Shot'.

———

There was a feel-good atmosphere among the Irish contingent who made it to the north-west edge of Detroit, a one-time boom-town which was depopulating at an extraordinary rate. Around Bloomfield, however, there was no evidence of such hardships: the impressive real estate around the country club left nobody in any doubt this was an area bucking the economic downturn.

Irish golf was also bucking a trend, feasting on good times. Harrington's back-to-back wins in the British Open — adding the championship at Royal Birkdale three weeks previously to the one he claimed at Carnoustie — had extended the glow to Graeme McDowell, a recent winner of the Scottish Open to add to the Ballantine's championship he had lifted earlier in the season, and to Darren Clarke, another player on a roll. Clarke had received a special invitation from the PGA of America to compete in the championship.

McDowell had enjoyed a top-20 finish in the Open at Birkdale that could have been even better, his efforts to win the Claret Jug undone by a horrendous outing in the third round when the wind blew him and his chances away.

The man known to one and all, friend and foe alike, as G-Mac, was familiar with American courses. He spent his college days as a hugely successful golfing scholar at the University of Alabama in

Birmingham where he was ranked the No. 1 college golfer in the United States. He had won six of 12 starts on the collegiate circuit and his 69.6 stroke average bettered the previous records of Luke Donald and Tiger Woods. He had made a seamless transition to life on the pro tour, taking with him the strange mix of the American Deep South to go with his Ulster accent.

That week, McDowell showed his diligence by tracking down a DVD of the 2004 Ryder Cup to see how the course played in competition and also scheduled a number of practice rounds with members of that winning European team. Among them were Harrington and Clarke.

In the WGC-Bridgestone Invitational the week before the PGA, McDowell had finished long before Fiji's Vijay Singh eked out a one-shot win over Lee Westwood and Stuart Apppleby. But McDowell's mind hadn't been on the tournament over the week in Akron. He had already started to shift his mindset to the challenge of Oakland Hills.

Between Birkdale and returning for the back-to-back tournaments in the United States, McDowell had returned home to Portrush on the Causeway Coast in Northern Ireland to, as he put it, 'unscramble' his mind.

The course which McDowell found at Oakland Hills was vastly different to the one which last staged a Major, the US Open, in 1996. Back then it measured 6,974 yards, but in the interim designer Rees Jones had been brought in to toughen up Donald Ross's original layout and it had been transformed into a course measuring 7,395 yards. Jones had lengthened 15 holes, narrowed several fairways, changed the depth and location of fairway bunkers on no fewer than 12 holes and made changes to greenside bunkers on eight holes. If Ben Hogan had likened it to a 'monster' following his 1951 US Open win, then McDowell and the other players who embarked on the quest to claim the 2008 US PGA were faced with an even tougher beast.

Harrington was one of those who believed players who had competed in the Ryder Cup four years beforehand would have an advantage. His reasoning was based on how the course actually played during the Ryder Cup compared to how it had played in the practice days. 'There were a lot of places you couldn't miss the pins and it was only by playing (the course) competitively could you tell . . . It had more to do with hitting the lines (off the tee) and how the holes changed.'

One incident from his initial play of the course stood out in Harrington's memory. 'I remember hitting the ball in the drain with a five-wood on the fifth (hole) and I got a rebuke from Bernhard Langer.' It was a mistake he didn't repeat in the Ryder Cup and, four years on, he brought that experience back with him to the course in the Detroit suburbs.

In the build-up to the PGA, Harrington was more gung-ho than his nature normally allowed. There were no injury scares, no problems with his focus. It didn't seem to matter either that the PGA, of all the Majors, was the one where he seemed to struggle the most: in nine previous appearances in the championship, his best finish had been tied-17th at Hazeltine National in 2002 and he had missed the cut on four occasions.

Such a record hardly seemed to matter to Harrington as he went about his business in the run-up to the 90th staging of the PGA. He was in exceptionally good spirits. 'I've nothing to report, apart from the fact that my body is falling apart,' he quipped midway through one practice round when the obligatory question on his health was put to him.

The gung-ho spirit was much in evidence. Of his chances, Harrington remarked: 'As results (in the PGA) would suggest over the years, I haven't really been ready to play . . . (Now) I know what I am doing. Whether I get it right or wrong is a different thing. But I do know what I am doing, which is very important. The results (in Majors) can be hit and miss, but the chances of me bringing my game (are better) . . . Whereas the PGA hasn't been my best, I don't see why it should be any different to any other Major.'

Apart from increased confidence, obviously brought about by his two British Open wins, there was an element of the wise old sage about Harrington on the eve of the PGA. 'My preparation wasn't great for the Open (at Birkdale), but I was comfortable because I'd played (in the Irish PGA). I used to believe that when I went to a Major I had to play to my very best. I put myself under too much pressure. I've realised now that whatever game I turn up with is the best game I have that week and I don't get as stressed on a Monday, Tuesday, Wednesday.'

———

The journey to the US PGA Championship at Oakland Hills had been an exhilarating ride for those players who had managed to play in the Majors of 2008; and for those watching! Trevor Immelman won the Green Jacket as US Masters champion at Augusta National Golf Club in April, just months after he had undergone surgery to remove a tumour; Tiger Woods had demonstrated unconquerable spirit when, literally on one good leg, he captured the US Open at Torrey Pines; and Pádraig Harrington, despite a wrist injury which hampered his preparation, had been imperious in successfully defending his British Open title at Royal Birkdale.

The 90th edition of the PGA Championship had a lot to live up to. Given the medical ailments which had troubled each of the year's Major winners, there were those who scanned the locker room in search of the next golfer to be afflicted. As Lee Westwood, still in search of a Major, quipped ahead of the tournament when asked if he had any injury to report, 'No, but I'm always capable of making one up . . . Oh, my neck!'

No player really wanted to be suffering from any ailment. The South Course — a par 70 of 7,395 yards — was an examination that required players to be in the whole of their health. The layout was more akin to that traditionally found at US Opens with fairways narrowed, the primary rough cut to a height of four inches and the greens running at 12½ on the Stimpmeter, the device used to measure the speed of the putting surfaces.

Of the European team that had conquered the course in its emphatic win over the United States in the Ryder Cup in 2004, eight players teed up in the PGA. The octet was part of a strong contingent that sought to end a drought of 78 years since a player from Europe had managed to get his name engraved on the prized Wanamaker trophy.

Ahead of the championship, Phil Mickelson — who'd famously driven out of bounds on the 18th hole when partnering Woods in the Ryder Cup — was installed as the favourite. But he was a fragile favourite. The previous week in the WGC-Bridgestone, he had bogeyed three of the last four holes.

The great conundrum was why European players had struggled so much in the US PGA down the years. Even when Bernhard Langer, Seve Ballesteros and Nick Faldo were in their prime, the title had stubbornly evaded their clutches.

Harrington, seeking to become just the fourth player in history to follow up a British Open win with a US PGA victory, had become the poster boy for Europe's renaissance. Just as he had ended the 60-year drought of an Irish Major winner dating back to Fred Daly in 1947 when he won the Open at Carnoustie in 2007, there was increased pressure on him to deliver as he set about ending an even longer drought since a European had won the PGA.

———

Sergio García didn't bother to shave ahead of Thursday's first round. He sported a healthy growth of stubble as he marched on to the first tee box and shook hands with two of golf's young pretenders, American Anthony Kim and Colombia's Camilo Villegas. Maybe the Spaniard's decision to leave the razor in the bathroom cabinet was to affirm to the younger players that he had been around the block a few more times. Who knows?

García made a point with an opening round of 69 that again launched him into a challenging position in a Major. In his near-decade long career as a professional, much of his life had been spent in pursuit of a Major. Many had believed it to be an inevitability, that he was destined for golfing greatness. But the US PGA was his 35th start as a professional in a Major and, despite several near misses, he had yet to claim the cherished silverware. Pádraig Harrington, as much as anyone, had seen to that.

There was an aura of confidence about García as he went about his first round business in the season's final Major. He liked the course, which always helped. In the 2004 Ryder Cup, he had won four and a half points from a possible five and he opened his account with a round — 15 pars, two birdies, one bogey — that showed maturity. He reined back his natural inclination to be aggressive, refusing to be tempted to aim at the flag all the time. 'Sometimes you've got to realise that you just can't go at them . . . It is hard, because we like to put an aggressive swing into everything we do. But sometimes you've got to realise what is right and what is wrong, to see if the gamble is worth it. I guess you learn as you get older.'

Age is but a number. García had exploded on to the pro scene in his maiden appearance in the us PGA at Medinah in 1999. A cocky teenager with great expectations, García — the son of a professional, Victor — knew he was good. He showed it too. At one point of that PGA debut, he hit a shot from the root of a tree trunk and ran after the ball as if he were an Olympic athlete, running and jumping with an exuberance rarely seen on the course. He chased down Tiger Woods that year and finished alone as runner-up. He was seen as the heir apparent, the one who would challenge the greatest player the game had ever seen.

García hadn't yet managed to win a Major, most dramatically losing out to Harrington in the play-off for the Claret Jug in the Open at Carnoustie in 2007. But he'd won the Players championship at Sawgrass in Florida in May 2008 — the so-called unofficial 'fifth Major' — which only served to instil new hope and belief in him.

On Thursday, the South Course proved to be every bit as unforgiving as any Major examination. As Westwood, not a player to be classified as a moaner or a whinger, remarked of the heavy rough which penalised any errant shots: 'It's horrendous . . . it hurts the guys that miss the fairways by two yards. It doesn't hurt the bombers who miss by 10 or 15 yards. It's stupid. I don't like it at all.'

Westwood's assertion didn't find universal approval, though. Mickelson called it 'challenging', but expanded: 'That's what we face in all the Majors. That's the patience factor, and one of the reasons why winning a Major is always more difficult.' He understood.

The first round was a real test. Apart from the heavy rough, alien to the usual PGA set-up, the greens firmed up considerably compared to their receptiveness in practice rounds. The upshot was a long, hard day at the office for the majority of players. As tends to happen, a number of them found a way to outwit the course's harshness. Sweden's Robert Karlsson, the tallest player on the PGA European Tour at the time, used all six foot four inches of his physique to muscle his way to a 68, two-under-par. It was a score matched only by the Indian, Jeev Milkha Singh.

Nobody was surprised to see Karlsson's name atop the first round leaderboard. He entered the season's closing Major with a distinction: he was the only player to have recorded top-10 finishes in the US Masters, US Open and British Open. 'I'm comfortable playing in the big events. Before, I tried too hard and pushed myself too much . . . so I always made a lot of mistakes. But this year the swing is better and I definitely feel a lot calmer and more content with life in general, not just on the golf course,' said Karlsson.

He elaborated that in the past he had tried 'to force results, tried to make things happen instead of just going out and playing.

I didn't play my own golf. I tried to almost play somebody else's golf and I couldn't see how my own golf was good enough to get around these courses.'

Karlsson's opening hole woke him up. His approach overshot the green into the rough and resulted in a bogey. His response was to birdie the next, and by the time he walked off the 11th green the tall Swede had got to four-under on his round. Back-to-back bogeys on the 14th and 15th threatened to derail him, but he covered the final three holes — the toughest on the course — in par-par-par to get in safely with a 68.

While Vijay Singh had entered the championship on the back of a win in the WGC-Bridgestone Invitational as a player fancied to perform well, it was his namesake Jeev Milkha who revealed after an opening 68 that he had had to wear a brace for almost a month in his efforts to curb the pain from an ankle tendon injury. It continued a rather bizarre streak of players in the Majors performing well with injuries, following Woods's win in the US Open and Harrington's in the British Open.

Of the injury, Singh explained: 'I've been getting a lot of physio treatment and it gets better . . . but you hit one of those shots out of the rough and I'm back to square one. I haven't played any practice rounds for the last seven weeks in the tournaments I've played and it has worked pretty well.'

The injury did not seem to have affected his ability to win. Singh won the Austrian Open the previous month and also won a tournament in Japan where he underwent an MRI scan and was told by his doctor to take a full month's rest. Having decided to ignore medical advice, he said: 'I decided if I'm going to play the PGA, then I'm going to push through this week . . . but the more drivers you hit, the more (the injury) comes back.'

Pádraig Harrington started his quest like a train. As the in-form player coming into the event on the back of his British Open triumph, he lived up to the expectations when he opened with a hat-trick of birdies. But that was as good as it got. As dark clouds gathered overhead, Harrington was called in after 14 holes, at which stage he was back to level par. He resumed after a lengthy rain delay and signed for a 71 which, he claimed, was 'a reasonable start in terms of the tournament, keeps you well in there, even though I feel a little frustrated that I left a few shots out there'.

Much of the frustration came on the greens, but Harrington showed he had retained his humour when asked if he was working on anything in particular. 'I was trying to calm down,' he quipped.

Laughter was probably the best medicine, for Harrington — who had played really well tee to green — struggled with the putter and watched a succession of birdie putts slide by the hole. One such instance came on the 15th hole, where a nine-foot birdie putt seemed for all the world like dropping, only to lip out. 'I really couldn't wait to get finished after that and it showed in my golf. I couldn't see anything really happening for me.'

When he got back to the locker room after a long and disrupted day, Harrington reflected that his situation wasn't entirely bad. Some players hadn't managed to finish their first rounds as darkness descended on the north-western suburbs of Detroit and, after all, he was just three shots adrift of the joint-leaders. 'It's all about staying patient for the first three days and I need to get my head around that,' he conceded.

Most bad Fridays are equated with the number 13. Friday the 13th *et al.* That's how it felt to Pádraig Harrington as he signed for a second round 74 for a five-over-par midway total of 145. That Friday — 8 August — was a bad one for the Irishman who, much like a marathon runner who hits the wall, seemed to have hit a wall of his own.

In that second round, fatigue hit the double British Open champion. The evidence was clear in the army golf, left-right-left, of his last few holes as he sprayed the ball into rough on either side of the fairway — anywhere, it seemed, but where the ball was supposed to go. 'I've just run out of steam. I did my best to be ready, but clearly I'm not. What can I say? The harder I tried, the worse it got. Obviously I'm having a (mental) hangover after winning the Open.'

On that Friday Harrington had everyone's sympathy. Not that he looked for it. That morning he had risen to a 5 am alarm call for his second round tee time, having had only a short sleep due to his weather-interrupted first round. Once he got out on to the course, he struggled to find or keep his focus. It was an old problem, and the fatigue — of winning at Royal Birkdale just weeks beforehand, of expectations — got to him.

If there was any solace for him to take on that day, it was that he had at least survived the midway cut. 'I'd love to just go with the flow . . . (but) when you're not mentally strong, it is hard to stop your mind from wandering away. I thought I was ready coming in, but I'm not. I don't have the focus and that's clearly a sign of being mentally fatigued.'

Harrington's second round — a 74 to follow Thursday's weather-interrupted 71 — contained the good, the bad and the plain ugly. The ugliest shots came towards the end, a pushed drive on the eighth (his 17th) that went so far right he got relief from a temporary internal fence close to the merchandise enclosure and then a pulled tee shot on the ninth (his finishing hole) that came to rest some 25 yards left of the green. Both indiscretions led to bogeys.

'I'd no ability to make my shots or to make anything happen,' claimed Harrington, of how his game went AWOL. 'I kept changing my mind mid-swing and that's why I hit some really bad shots at the end . . . (but) I'm quite happy with the consequences of winning the Open if this is it. I realise it takes a lot to come back out and try to perform in a major two weeks after winning one. Maybe they are too close.' The two-week gap between the British Open and the US PGA was the shortest between any of the Majors: there was a seven-week gap between the US Masters and the US Open, and a three-week break between the US Open and the British Open.

After his round, Harrington ditched plans to work on elements of his game that he felt required work and instead headed back to his rented house contemplating a long sleep. 'If I could sleep for 24 hours, I would,' he remarked. 'I'm struggling to hold my attention and focus and that's a sign you're tired . . . Maybe a good sleep overnight and I'll be better tomorrow. Who knows?'

Harrington hadn't thrown in the towel after his second round. It simply was not in the man's nature to do that. Listening to him on that Friday, he sounded tired and didn't seem as if he had the energy for the fight ahead on one of golf's toughest examinations. It was only natural to start looking towards others as potential champions.

One of the more likely pretenders to a crown won by the absent Tiger Woods the previous year at Southern Hills Country Club in Tulsa, Oklahoma, was Justin Rose. As a golfer, the South African-born Englishman was an enigma. On a course described as 'nasty' and 'very difficult' by his peers, Rose moved into contention with a second round 67 for 140, level par, that enabled him to leapfrog players with all the zeal of a child in the playground.

Other players walked to the recorder's hut mentally battered and bruised, as if they had gone 12 rounds with Mike Tyson. The course, tough as it was, had been made even tougher by a swirling wind, but Rose was very much in the mix after a round in which he used his putter like a magic wand. He required just 25 putts in his second round.

The enigma was that putting had been his nemesis all year. Rose ranked 197th in putting on the US Tour heading into the PGA Championship, but performed brilliantly on the firm and pernickety greens to reach the midway stage just one shot adrift of the midway leader, the American, J. B. Holmes. Rose was joined in a share of second place by Ben Curtis and Charlie Wi.

An indication of the ferocious nature of the Oakland Hills greens was the failure of Vijay Singh, then the world's fourth ranked player and a winner in Akron the previous week, to survive the midway cut. The Fijian five-putted his final hole. Others to succumb included Colin Montgomerie, the eight-time European Tour Order of Merit winner, and world No. 8 Adam Scott, while the first round co-leader Karlsson took nine shots more than his opening effort to finish on 145, the same score as Harrington.

All of which made Rose's 67 — the joint-best round of the day with Curtis — look better. Had he finally emerged as a viable

Major contender? 'It's been a waiting game, I suppose, to start putting well again. All year parts of my game have been up and down, but putting's one area I haven't had any confidence with. It's been a matter of waiting for the confidence to come back, to believe in yourself again. That's how fickle it is, I suppose.'

———

Rose's putting wasn't the only fickle element in the 90th PGA Championship. The weather, too, proved to have a life of its own. Although the third round started that morning under clear skies, the arrival of dark clouds in the afternoon forced officials to suspend play at 2.16 pm, just over half an hour before leader J. B. Holmes was scheduled to start.

He never got to play that day.

No fewer than three heavy thunderstorms left their mark which led originally to a suspension of play and then to its abandonment for the day. Six players — David Toms, Henrik Stenson, Ben Curtis, Justin Rose, Charlie Wi and Holmes — never got to hit a ball, while the majority of the field marked their balls where they lay on the course when the siren sounded.

Some players, though, managed to finish. One of them was Andrés Romero, the young Argentine who had shown Major intent in the 2007 British Open at Carnoustie, only to fall a shot short of the play-off that featured Pádraig Harrington and Sergio García. One of the early starters and one of the few to complete their rounds before the weather closed in, Romero shot a course record-equalling 65. It proved to be the best round of the championship, one which moved him from tied-48th at the start of the third round up into the top-10.

———

If anyone was grateful for the weather closing in on the Saturday, it was Pádraig Harrington. Fatigued at the midpoint on the Friday evening, his failure to complete his third round proved to be a blessing in disguise. It gave him a chance to recharge his batteries and the 4 am alarm call on Sunday heralded a new dawn as far as the player was concerned.

The cocktail of thunder, lightning and heavy rain which hit the championship on Saturday had the effect of taking much of the firmness out of the greens. If a player managed to keep his ball on the straight and narrow off the tee, avoiding the clinging rough, then the greens were far more receptive. Harrington, who had appeared tired beyond belief when retiring to his rented house on Indian Mound West on Friday evening, was like a spring lamb as he completed his third round on Sunday morning.

On Friday night, Harrington and his physical therapist Dale Richardson had sat down to discuss why he felt so drained. The player had felt it was mental fatigue brought on by a number of factors. Richardson was of the opinion that it had to do with dehydration. 'And that (explained) the lack of co-ordination (at the end of the second round),' said Harrington. 'So it gave me something to focus on. I focused on rehydrating myself.'

It worked.

If his job on Saturday had been left incomplete, he finished it in some style when he resumed his third round early the following morning. Harrington had four birdies on the back nine and, when it came to totting up the numbers, he signed for a third round 66 that put him on 211, one-over, and left him in tied-fourth. He was in the mix in a Major again, and just three shots adrift of the 54-hole leader Ben Curtis. He had been cast in the role of pursuer, just the way he liked it.

Harrington and Curtis had developed a friendship in their time on tour. The other thing they had in common was they were both Major champions. Curtis had come out of the blue to win the British Open in 2003 — on his first ever appearance in a Major — and Harrington had followed his footsteps when claiming the Claret Jug at Carnoustie in 2007.

Unlike Harrington, who had managed to play a number of holes on Saturday, Curtis had spent his time on the range and in the clubhouse without ever getting to the course. He was one of six players who were required to play a full 18 holes of the third round when he returned to the course on Sunday for a 7.40 am tee time and shot a 68 for 208 that left him atop the leaderboard. Holmes and Sweden's Henrik Stenson, on 209, were the only other players under par.

Curtis wore a Detroit Lions cap — part of a sponsorship deal he had with American Football's NFL which had him wearing the colours of various teams as the regular PGA Tour pitched from one city to another — which earned him added support from the Michigan galleries.

Justin Rose's enigmatic form returned to haunt him as a third round 74 saw him slump down the field into tied-13th and removed from the main drama.

———

The green staff at Oakland Hills worked wonders to have the course playable for a marvellously chaotic Sunday, where play literally started shortly after first light and came to an end as dusk beckoned. There was no evidence of the heavy thunderstorms of the previous day where ponds had appeared where the designer Donald Ross had never intended water hazards.

Pádraig Harrington was three strokes adrift of the leader Ben Curtis as he went through his warm-up for the final round. As he had proved at Carnoustie the previous year when making up a six-stroke deficit in the final round, the number of shots — in this case three — was only one factor. The other was the number of players in between. And the fact that only J. B. Holmes and Henrik Stenson were sandwiched between him and Curtis gave the Irishman an added pep to his step as he headed to the first tee for the final round.

One man who took an added interest as Harrington set about his quest for a third Major title inside 13 months was Nick Faldo. The Englishman — captain of the European Ryder Cup team at Valhalla in Kentucky later that season — had six Majors of his own in an honour-laden career and he had some words of advice for the Irishman. 'You forget about running on empty. Monday is the day to feel exhausted. This is a mental test and a strategy test and it is all about solid ball-striking because there's no margin for error.'

What must Sergio García have thought on that long Sunday? The Spaniard was on the first tee as Harrington and caddie Ronan Flood walked on to the teeing ground, both smiling and set for another episode in an extraordinary journey. Flood's days as a pencil-pushing, laptop-pounding, number-crunching bank official were in the past as he earned a reputation as one of the most reliable caddies on the tour and an able lieutenant for his player.

Of all the players on tour, García — the vanquished from their British Open play-off at Carnoustie — had suffered most from Harrington's emergence as a multiple Major champion. García smiled to the Irishman on the tee, but there was little interaction thereafter as they got into the heat of another battle for a Major, this time for the Wanamaker trophy. Curtis may have had an edge going into the final round, but Harrington and García, more than anyone, knew fortune favoured the brave. The game was on.

Harrington was very much up for the challenge. The man who looked drained just two days earlier after he finished his second round was refreshed and full of vigour. He had made the most of Saturday's rain-interrupted third round — he had completed nine holes before the klaxon sounded to alert players of a danger-ous weather front — when he found a quiet area in the locker room and took a nap. If other players shook their heads at the sight of Harrington curled up asleep on the floor, the player himself was oblivious. He needed all the rest he could get.

The early charge in the final round was made by García, a player desperate to rid himself of the tag nobody wanted: 'best player never to have won a Major'. García birdied the first and eagled the second (hitting a nine-iron approach to the par 5 to four feet) to move to three-under and a great up-and-down from greenside rough on the ninth enabled him to assume the lead (on three-under) after Curtis suffered back-to-back bogeys on the eighth and ninth holes to fall back to two-under.

On a cool day, with a swirling wind and occasional rain showers adding to the final round test, Curtis — the 2003 British Open champion at Royal St George's — got an up close view on the very first hole of how Oakland Hills could bite. J. B. Holmes, the longest driver on the US Tour, took a triple-bogey seven on the first after driving into trees and unwisely attempting to chip back out on to the fairway, only to leave his ball in a worse spot. He was forced to take a penalty drop, and that triple-bogey was followed by a run of bogey-bogey as his bid for a first Major disintegrated.

Harrington stayed focused — having suffered a bogey-five on the fifth where his six-iron approach from 191 yards flew the green — and showed his ability to grind out scores, getting up and down from a 50-yard bunker shot on the sixth for a birdie, and then rolling in a 20 footer for birdie on the 10th that moved him to one-under and two strokes adrift of leader García, who was four-under on his round at that juncture. It was very much game on between old adversaries García and Harrington, with Curtis and Stenson also still in the mix.

———

On the Sunday of any Major, it is all about what happens on the back nine. That is when the final leg of the journey takes place and you discover what is under a player's skin. It is when the heart thumps a million times faster and when the muscles tighten. It is when the hard questions need to be answered. On such occasions, as the grand prize looms ever closer, Harrington's eyes are the giveaway. They look like they are about to pop out of his head. He is in a zone.

———

Harrington made his move as soon as he turned for home. On the 10th he rolled in a 20 footer for birdie. On the 12th the task was easier: he sank a five footer. On the 13th he rolled in a 10 footer for birdie. He had moved into a tie for the lead with García. Behind them, Curtis knew that something was afoot. The roars from ahead dwarfed anything that his tail-end group made.

On the 15th, García probably got a hint that the golfing gods were again using him as a plaything. His approach shot looked perfect. It was. But the ball hit the cup and then hit the pin, and rolled 10 feet away from the hole. He two-putted for par and was left to wonder what might have been if his ball hadn't spun away from the flagstick.

The par 4 16th had earned a reputation as the signature hole at Oakland Hills. García and Harrington found the fairway with their tee shots, but from there the real work had to be done: finding the green. Both failed. García's approach came up short and right of the green and bounced back into the water. Harrington's eight-iron approach was pulled into a greenside bunker.

Flood, the caddie-cum-confidant, felt it was time to have a word in Harrington's ear. 'You can't get into a match play situation,' he warned his man.

Harrington heeded the words, and admitted: 'Up to that I was engaged in a match play situation. Because Sergio was in the lead,

I was chasing. I did tell myself all along, even when he had a three-shot lead or a two-shot lead, that it could be just one hole that could change that around. I was trying to stay patient and hang in there, trying to take my chances. But there's no question I had one eye on Sergio.'

Harrington had demonstrated superlative bunker play throughout his round. Time and time again he had got up and down. On the sixth. On the seventh. On the ninth. On the 16th, he splashed out to 15 feet and then holed a vicious right-to-left breaking putt to save par. García, too, got up and down from the drop zone — but for bogey — and the pair walked on to the 17th tee locked together in a share of the lead with Curtis (who simultaneously bogeyed the 15th) on two-under-par.

By the time they walked off the 17th green, Harrington had it all to himself. Earlier in the day, Sweden's Fredrik Jacobson had recorded a hole-in-one on the par 3. What García would have given to replicate that feat; and he nearly did. The roars had only eased to acknowledge Harrington's five-iron tee shot to 10 feet when García responded by hitting his to four feet.

Harrington's putter was on fire; he holed his birdie putt. García missed; his ball lipped out as if an invisible hand was inside the tin cup.

Perhaps there is something of a thespian in Harrington, for no golfer does drama quite like him. On the 72nd hole, Harrington drove into a fairway bunker and his recovery shot finished up in the heaviest rough on the golf course. With 143 yards to the flag, he hit a seven-iron approach to 15 feet on the elevated green and holed the par putt. García, who missed his subsequent par putt, seemed to be in a state of shock.

Harrington, the British Open champion of 2007 and 2008, had added the PGA — a third Major — to his list of honours. He seemed less surprised than anyone. As he left the green, he kissed his wife Caroline, mother Breda and sons Paddy and Ciarán, and then plonked a kiss on the Wanamaker trophy. Harrington's final round 66 to add to his third round 66 finished on 277, two shots clear of García and Curtis.

For a guy deemed almost too nice, Harrington — for a third time — had shown an assassin's instincts down the stretch. 'Did I feel an edge (on García)?' he wondered. 'I felt an edge in my experience. I felt an edge in terms of my ability to take an opportunity when it comes around.'

He had again proven to be one of the best closers in the game. Tigeresque almost.

———

The scary eyes were gone the next morning as Harrington — in casual mode — sat with Ciarán on his knees and his wife Caroline double-checked that all the bags were packed and ready as they prepared to take a family holiday in North Carolina.

As a boy starting to hit shots at Stackstown Golf Club, Harrington had only dared to dream about winning Majors. A matter of hours after claiming his third, he sat by the poolside in the back garden of that house in Indian Mound West in the township of Bloomfield, Michigan. He had moved into new territory as a golfing great.

He found it hard to get his head around the notion that he was, indeed, a golfing great. 'Having won three Majors in the modern era, and the players I compare myself to and the Majors they have won, I have to start accepting I am who I am. I've probably been the best player in Europe for six years, but over that time I haven't really shouted it from the tree tops. Now, I've got to get to grips with who I am as a player, and where I am. I've won as many Majors now as Phil Mickelson, Ernie Els and Vijay Singh. And they are considered that next tier behind Tiger. I'm younger than the three of them, and that says a lot. I'm the youngest and I have three Majors. I feel like my game is going from strength to strength.'

Harrington pointed out that as he has progressed to each level throughout his career, he has always found it difficult until he got to the comfort zone where suddenly it all came good. 'You know, the next level is just staying here. I've already proved I can win Majors. I'm not turning around here and saying I'm going to break it down and change everything. I don't need to. But I do need to try and improve, to get more sustainability . . . and probably more sustainability in normal tournaments, in believing I am a guy who has won three Majors.

'I can hit all the shots. I have all the belief . . . but you'd be surprised at how much hard work I make it for myself. I've always had the ability to hole putts, to get into that zone . . . The best part of golf is when I have to make things happen. It is what I look for, what I enjoy, what I relish. To make things happen . . . I've always had good internal belief, but I need to have that ability to walk on to the first tee, puff out my chest and say, I'm here. It's something I have never had.'

Chapter 6 ∿

GIANT STRIDES FROM CAUSEWAY COAST TO PEBBLE BEACH

110th US Open Championship, Pebble Beach
Links, California, USA

June 2010

On the morning of 24 May, a Monday, Graeme McDowell woke up, not to meet a scheduled early morning tee time, a function seen as part and parcel of any profess-ional's life, but to source important information. He switched on his computer and discovered that the golfing gods had been kind. The Ulsterman had put the search engine on the official world golf rankings and found that he had remained inside the world's top-50. It meant he could book his flight ticket to Pebble Beach for the 110th US Open Championship.

Nobody needed to tell the man known as G-Mac that fate had dealt him a good hand. It could just as easily have swung the other way. The previous day, McDowell had finished tied-28th in the BMW PGA Championship over the West Course at Wentworth. The tournament had been won by Englishman Simon Khan, ranked 471st in the world in the week before the PGA European

Tour's flagship event. Khan had only got a place in the field as a reserve after a number of late withdrawals. His win was symbolic of the thin line, not just between success and failure, but of being a competitor or an observer.

As Khan had marched to a career-defining victory on that Sunday, McDowell wondered if he would live to regret a final round that reminded him of the theory of Murphy's Law. 'It was one of those days where everything that could go wrong, did go wrong,' he remarked. Not quite everything, though. After a run of three successive bogeys from the 14th hole, McDowell conjured up an eagle on the 17th that seemed more like damage limitation than something to celebrate. He signed for a 74, in tied-28th, and made his way to the magnificent clubhouse with his manager, Conor Ridge. He couldn't have known how important that eagle would be in the great scheme of things.

In the clubhouse, McDowell and Ridge had a chat about his future schedule. International Qualifying for the US Open was to be held at Walton Heath the next day, a lottery that nevertheless had proven life-changing for New Zealander Michael Campbell who had taken a similar path *en route* to a remarkable US Open win at Pinehurst No. 2 in 2005, but McDowell had a dilemma. Would he play or not? If he managed to stay inside the world's top-50 when the following day's updated world rankings were announced, then he would be in the field for Pebble Beach. If he wasn't, his only other route was through the qualifying tournament.

On that Sunday evening, McDowell and Ridge reached a decision. He wouldn't play Walton Heath. If he remained inside the world's top-50, well and good. If he didn't, then he would change his schedule and add the BMW International on the European Tour in place of the US Open. 'If I don't get in, it's not the end of my summer,' the player told his manager, aware of the gamble he had taken.

The situation was complicated by the fact that the world rankings were also dependent on what happened on the PGA Tour that Sunday night, where a number of players competing in the Byron Nelson Classic had an opportunity to leapfrog McDowell in the rankings. It was down to the wire. Neither Brian Gay nor Scott Verplank could have known it, but their play on the 18th hole of the final round could have ended McDowell's US Open challenge before it ever got started. If the two had birdied that closing hole, McDowell would have slipped out of the world's top-50.

When McDowell turned on his computer on the Monday morning and checked the world rankings, he allowed himself a smile.

'Okay, I've got the US Open.'

Then, an afterthought: 'Wow!' He had scraped in. World No. 49. 'Wow!'

————

Graeme McDowell didn't twiddle his thumbs after getting into the field for the US Open. Having given the US Open International Qualifying at Walton Heath a wide berth, a wise decision as it turned out, the Ulsterman made his way to the Wales Open at Celtic Manor Resort in the city of Newport, outside Cardiff.

It was a place he knew well. McDowell had lived in the area for a number of years in his earlier days on tour — when dating a Welsh girl — and he was also familiar with the course at Celtic Manor, the host venue for the Ryder Cup match between the United States and Europe later in the season. When McDowell shot a closing round 63 to win the Wales Open, it did two things: it gave his prospects of making Colin Montgomerie's Europe team a shot in the arm; and it sent the Ulsterman off to Pebble Beach in fine fettle. After the frustration of that final round in the BMW PGA at Wentworth, the cards had started to fall his way. His confidence was up.

As McDowell admitted on the Sunday night of his Wales Open win, his fifth career win on the PGA European Tour, 'I feel like I'm in the form of my life right now and I really feel I have a big event in me.'

He couldn't have known just how prophetic his own words would be, but the links at Pebble Beach — and a place in history — beckoned for the son of the Causeway Coast.

———

Geoff Ogilvy described Pebble Beach as one of the 'spiritual' homes of American golf, not so much because it was one of golf's founding influences — it wasn't — but rather for the type of championship it invariably provided whenever the USGA came calling every few years for the US Open. 'It's symbolic of American golf and you've had three of the biggest legends win,' remarked the Aussie, who had earned his US Open win at Winged Foot in 2006.

Just how Tom Kite — the winner in 1992 — felt about being the odd man out in Ogilvy's assessment of past winners was probably immaterial, but for sure in producing winners of the calibre of Jack Nicklaus (1972), Tom Watson (82) and Tiger Woods (2000), the famed and majestically located links on the Monterey Peninsula hard by the Pacific had produced some of the sport's greatest champions in an examination considered second to none.

Each year at the second Major of the season, traditionally two months after the US Masters and a month before the British Open, the USGA set out with the aim of presenting the hardest test of any of the four Majors. As Tom O'Toole, the championship chairman at Pebble Beach put it: 'The US Open should be the most rigorous, the most difficult and yet fair test in championship golf, an examination which tests both the players' physical capabilities, which includes all shot-making, but also tests the players' mental capabilities and tenacities . . . well-executed shots rewarded, poorly executed shots penalised.'

For the third year in a row, the USGA had brought the US Open to what is deemed to be a public links, following on from Torrey Pines (2008) and Bethpage (2009). Yet there was a mystique about Pebble Beach which didn't resonate with the previous two venues. What was it? It's location? Ernie Els, cast in the role of principal onlooker to the master class provided by Tiger Woods a decade previously, observed: 'As a venue, I don't think you can get a better one any place in the world.'

Stewart Cink, the British Open champion of 2009, was a bit of a sentimentalist when it came to the links. 'If St Andrews is the home of golf, I think Pebble Beach kind of feels like the home of American golf. I know other places probably disagree with that, like Pinehurst would probably lay claim to that, but Pebble Beach feels like the home of championship golf. It predates even the US Open (being) played here, (starting) with the Crosby Clambake. It has a real sense of history . . . so many shots we've seen over the years by Watson, Nicklaus, Tiger.'

A queue of other players offered sentiments. Pádraig Harrington, a regular visitor to the AT&T where he traditionally teed it up alongside Irish businessman J. P McManus, remarked: 'It seems a little bit like the home of the US Open. We come back every 10 years or so, but it is a little bit like St Andrews (the British Open) going back there every five years. It's one of those venues that stands out in people's minds. Everybody remembers Tom Watson chipping in (in 82), Tiger winning by 15 shots (in 2000), Tom Kite getting to 10-under-par. It is more synonymous for the US Open than any other.'

Watson, whose chip-in birdie in the final round of the 1982 US Open was one of those shots heard around the world, didn't need any convincing about the magical appeal of the links. 'It's got a lot of stories, a lot of stories about it . . . it has a rich fabric of golf and the US Open should come back. It's a wonderful venue.'

Although hailing from Kansas, Watson — apart from his US Open victory — had a rich association with Pebble Beach. When he attended Stanford University in San Francisco, he played the links more than a dozen times and he recalled playing the US PGA in 1977 when 'we had cracks in the fairway and it was really, really dry'. Of course, Watson had one record all of his own: he was the only player to have played in each one of the five US Opens staged on the course, courtesy of a special invitation extended to him in 2010 by the USGA.

There have been many famous shots hit at Pebble Beach: Watson's chip-in, of course, from deep rough in 1982 to stun Nicklaus; then there was Nicklaus's own one-iron which hit the flag on that same 17th hole on his way to a third US Open title in 72; Tom Kite's pitch in a howling wind on the seventh *en route* to victory in 1992, and Woods's slash with a seven-iron out of the deep rough on the sixth to reach the par 5 in two in 2000.

But the best shot of all? How about Jack Lemmon's in the 1981 Bing Crosby National Pro-Am. The actor's opening tee shot flew off the toe of his driver, zinged over the heads of the spectators, found a gap through the trees and finished up in his own house!

Ah, the magical appeal of Pebble Beach.

In the practice days leading up to the 110th US Open, it was rather appealing to watch players react as they moved from the 17th green to the 18th tee. Invariably, the players would stop and simply inhale a deep breath as they took in the scene on the cliff top down to the Pacific Ocean where the waves crashed on to the rocks and sea lions lazed in the sunshine.

On Tuesday evening, one group lingered longer than most. Rory McIlroy had become acquainted with the famed links for the first time the previous day. Up to then his only link to the course had come by playing it on his Sony PlayStation — when he frequently shot rounds in the 50s as he aggressively went for the par 5s in two — but, in the flesh, he had discovered it to be a different beast.

As McIlroy, Graeme McDowell and Ian Poulter left the 17th green, Poulter pulled a camera from his bag and insisted that all of the players and their entourage get into a shot for posterity. It was Poulter's first visit to Pebble Beach, having never ventured there for the AT&T National Pro-Am, the customary early season stop on the regular PGA Tour each year. 'It's better than everything I read. I mean, you try and get some visual, but there's nothing like playing it for real. It's very different than what it obviously looks like on a video game.'

The three players were in form and generally considered capable of putting an end to a long drought in the US Open since a European player had triumphed. Tony Jacklin's win in 1970 at Hazeltine National was an age before any of them had even been born. And, of the trio, many observers had ear-marked McIlroy as the one most likely to end the long drought.

McIlroy had made his debut in the US Open at Bethpage on Long Island, New York, the previous year and secured a top-10 finish in a weather-interrupted championship won by American Lucas Glover. On that occasion he had come in a little under the radar. There was no such stealth for the tournament at Pebble Beach. McIlroy had spectacularly won the Quail Hollow Championship on the PGA Tour in May and the US audience had woken up to what Irish, British and European observers had known in his amateur and fledgling professional days: his was a special talent.

In the days before the championship, as he went about practice rounds with his good friend McDowell, McIlroy was asked how close he was to winning a Major? 'I've got to be going into this tournament thinking that I can win, that I have a chance to win.

If I can get into position going into the weekend, I should have a chance . . . Maybe in a couple of years I'll hopefully be a bit more advanced in my career to say, yeah, I think it's time, that I'm ready to win a Major.'

Anyone who followed McIlroy and McDowell in the days before the championship started at Pebble Beach would have been drawn by the meticulous attention to detail of both players, and of their willingness to demonstrate shots from greenside rough to each other and how they should be played. Interestingly, in a number of instances, it was McIlroy who was the demonstrator. McDowell watched, listened and learned.

As ever, Tiger Woods, the greatest golfer of his generation, demanded a lot of attention in the days running up to the championship. No one in the starting field had as many Majors as he did, 14. No one in US Open history had ever decimated a field the way he had, by 15 strokes at Pebble Beach in 2000. No one had ever looked as invincible, in their prime.

Woods was no longer in his prime as he counted down to the start of the 110th US Open. Sure, he entered the Major as the world's No. 1 golfer for a straight 206th week, but the marital infidelities that had taken Woods away from the sports and business pages on to the cover of tabloids and celebrity websites meant his image — and his game — had changed. The aura of invincibility was gone.

Woods was a man still regaining control of his life as he prepared for the championship, his second Major since his comeback, after he took time out to attend rehab after his succession of extramarital affairs became public.

Woods had finished fourth in the US Masters — behind Phil Mickelson — in April, but suffered a neck injury in the Players tournament at Sawgrass in May which had hampered his build-up to the US Open. 'The neck is better. It's not where I want it, but it is better. No doubt. It gets sore from time to time but I can recover for the next day. And I haven't had any days where I couldn't go (and play) the next day. That's a big step in the right direction,' he said as he went in search of a 15th Major in his obsessive pursuit of the record 18 held by Jack Nicklaus.

When Woods won the US Open at Pebble Beach in 2000, he seemed to be playing a different course to everyone else. He ran away with it. Asked how he perceived the challenge 10 years on, Woods responded: 'Well, it's the toughest rough we play all year. It's the narrowest fairways, the hardest greens, the trickiest pins. Other than that, yeah, it's pretty simple . . . as far as the set-up is concerned. You have to be patient. You have to understand it's a long haul. You're not going to make a lot of birdies and the whole idea is not to make any big numbers.'

———

The cool weather front in the run-up to the 110th US Open and in the first round took the players by surprise. Pádraig Harrington, who had undergone arthroscopic knee surgery less than a month previously, felt the need to contact his clothing sponsor Kartel to FedEx extra sweaters out to the West Coast. He was suitably attired by the time he walked to the first tee box early on Thursday.

Harrington was one part of the morning marquee three-ball that also featured Korean Y.E. Yang and local hero Phil Mickelson. 'Happy birthday, Phil!' was a common throwaway to the left-handed American as Mickelson, smiling as ever and dressed all in black akin to the dress code of the original 'Black Knight' Gary Player, made his way to the tee. Harrington, hands tucked into his pockets to offset the cool breeze coming in off the Pacific, made his farmer's jaunt in Mickelson's shadow. Yang walked behind them.

Mickelson had won the US Masters at Augusta National in April, his fourth career Major. Between the three of them, they possessed eight Major titles. Mickelson had four; Harrington had three; and Yang had one, a win fashioned in the US PGA at Hazeltine National in 2009 where he fended off Tiger Woods down the stretch.

Once, the actor Bob Hope had likened Pebble Beach to 'Alcatraz with grass', an inference to its capacity to hurt players. The links possessed many hazards, apart from the small greens and the heavy rough. The bunkers were among the toughest to be found on any course; and, of course, there was the Pacific Ocean itself which came into play on the run of holes from the eighth to the 10th — part of the course known as the Cliffs of Doom, the hardest stretch of par 4s in professional golf — and also on the 18th hole.

Among the earlier starts on Thursday, the play of the three Major champions was to provide a glimpse of the challenge that every player in the field would face. Mickelson went through his entire round without making a birdie, and his play of the 17th and 18th holes revived memories of an old television commercial he did for Ford which asked, 'What Will Phil Do Next?' The advertisement was based on Mickelson's propensity to hit wild shots, and on the 17th he carved his tee shot into Carmel Bay, and then on the 18th he cut a three-wood approach down to the rocks and onwards into the ocean.

The scores reflected the struggles of the three men. Harrington signed for a 73, Yang for a 73, and Mickelson for a 75. Pebble Beach looked like paradise, but there was a hellish element too.

Nine players managed to shoot sub-par rounds on the first day. England's Paul Casey, Zimbabwean Brendan de Jonge and American Shaun Micheel, the US PGA champion of 2003, shot 69s which left them a stroke clear of six players — which included Ian Poulter — on 70.

Poulter, one of the snappiest dressed golfers on tour and a player with his own clothing line, was also part of the early wave of players and had done his day's work by the time the likes of Tiger Woods and a certain Graeme McDowell were just starting theirs.

The clothes horse was part of an exceptionally strong English contingent which included Paul Casey and Luke Donald. Although it was Poulter's first competitive round over the links, he admitted to falling in love with it at first sight. 'You have to stay patient or you will be going home pretty quickly. If you get a little bit impatient and take on a shot you shouldn't, you can make triple-bogey very quickly,' observed Poulter. 'I'm not interested in a winning score, just in playing golf. It's irrelevant to me what score wins as long as I finish one shot better than anybody else.'

Graeme McDowell had been a little tetchy in the days before the 110th US Open got under way. Those around him — his father Kenny and manager Conor Ridge — only smiled when such tetchiness became a character trait. It meant only one thing, a good thing: the player was in form and he was aware that he was striking the ball well.

The Ulsterman's place in the field might have been in doubt right up to the time the world rankings were released on the Monday after the BMW PGA at Wentworth, but he had been around enough Majors and other big-time occasions — going back to his Walker Cup days — to know that tournaments weren't won on the first day. He knew it was about hanging tough for three and a half rounds and that the real work was done down the finishing straight of the final round.

McDowell opened his US Open with a 71, a score that got him into contention. He was in a share of 10th place — alongside Luke Donald, David Toms and Dustin Johnson — and, on a day when neither Phil Mickelson nor Tiger Woods managed to make a birdie, the first time since the first round of the 2003 Masters that both players had failed to do so, McDowell could feel content with his efforts.

In his time on tour, McDowell — like Rory McIlroy, an avid Manchester United fan — had pursued perfection and shown a ruthlessness in his efforts to make it to the top. He had changed management companies, from International Sports Management to Horizon Sports, at the end of the 2007 season and put in place a team of people around him who worked hard and strove to get the best out of the player.

One of that team was Kenny Comboy, recognised as one of the best caddies on tour. In the first round, Comboy had to work

The Pioneer. With a swing developed on the famed links of Royal Portrush, Fred Daly became the first Irishman to win a Major when he captured the Open championship at Hoylake, outside Liverpool, in 1947. The Ulsterman was shouldered off the 18th green after his triumph. Nobody could have imaged it would be 60 years before another Irish golfer would end the famine. (© *Getty Images*)

A dream come true. His wife Caroline bends to lift up their son Patrick as Pádraig Harrington soaks in the reality of his breakthrough Major triumph in the 2007 Open. The Dubliner's sense of joyful disbelief, hands behind his head and wide smile, is in marked contrast to the grief of Sergio García who appears devastated. (© *Inpho Photography*)

Smile, please. Not a ladybird in sight as Pádraig Harrington sits on the edge of a bunker by the 18th green at Carnoustie as the world's media jockey for position to zoom their cameras on 'The Champion Golfer of the Year'. (© *Inpho Photography*)

Fortitude personified. Pádraig Harrington had put two balls into the Barry Burn on the 18th hole of his final round of the Open at Carnoustie in 2007 but demonstrated strong mental fortitude — and an unwavering trust in his swing — to chip over the hazard to get up and down for a double-bogey six which got him into a play-off with Spain's Sergio García. The pitch became the iconic shot of Harrington's triumph. (© *Press Association*)

Home is the hero. His head may still be in the clouds after his breakthrough Major triumph, but Pádraig Harrington touches down on *terra firma* at Weston Airfield, outside Dublin, with the Claret Jug — one of sport's true status symbols. (© *Inpho Photography*)

On the par 5 17th hole of his final round at Royal Birkdale, Pádraig Harrington hit a
wonder shot with a five-wood which bounced over the bunker guarding the green
and ran up to the hole. He made the eagle putt to put the icing on the cake of his
back-to-back titles. (© *Getty Images*)

Ice, Ice, Baby. Pádraig Harrington's defence of his Open title at Royal Birkdale in 2008 was threatened after he sustained a wrist injury during a practice session at his home in Rathmichael, Co. Dublin. His pre-championship practice was limited to chipping and putting, with caddie Ronan Flood carrying the few necessary clubs, and applying ice — wrapped in a tea towel — to his right wrist. (© *Inpho Photography*)

Strolling to greatness. Greg Norman, one of golf's modern legends, walks in the shadow of Pádraig Harrington whose successful defence enabled him to join an elite club of back-to-back Open champions. The Irishman became only the seventh player since the Second World War to perform the feat, joining Tiger Woods, Tom Watson, Lee Trevino, Arnold Palmer, Peter Thomson and Bobby Locke. (© *Inpho Photography*)

Back-to-back champion. On returning the Claret Jug to the R&A prior to the 137th Open at Royal Birkdale, Pádraig Harrington had joked the governing body were only minding it for him. He made good on the promise, much to the delight of the large crowds of supporters who had travelled across the Irish Sea to witness his successful defence. (© *Inpho Photography*)

Eyes on the ball. Pádraig Harrington hitting his tee shot into the par 3 ninth hole in the first round of the 2008 US PGA Championship at Oakland Hills Country Club, outside Detroit, in Michigan. (© *Inpho Photography*)

Moment of victory. After a duel down the stretch with old adversary Sergio García, Pádraig Harrington became the first European player — since US-based Scotsman Tommy Armour in 1930 — to win the US PGA Championship. Harrington's par putt save on the 18th green gave him a third Major title inside a golden 14-month period. (© *Inpho Photography*)

Sealed with a kiss. Pádraig Harrington poses with the Wanamaker trophy — the largest of all the Major trophies — after winning the 90th US PGA Championship at Oakland Hills Country Club. (© *Inpho Photography*)

Last man standing. Graeme McDowell raises his eyes to the heavens after sealing victory in the 2010 US Open at Pebble Beach. He joined an exclusive club featuring Jack Nicklaus, Tom Watson, Tom Kite and Tiger Woods who triumphed at the famed links on the Monterey Peninsula. (© *Inpho Photography*)

On top of the world. Graeme McDowell is impervious to the beach walkers below at Carmel Bay as he gives his entire attention to a putt on the ninth hole in the final round of the 2010 US Open at Pebble Beach links on his way to a maiden Major title. (© *Inpho Photography*)

The numbers don't lie. Northern Ireland's Graeme McDowell can barely contain his smile as he poses with the US Open trophy in front of the giant leaderboard by the 18th green at Pebble Beach where the hole-by-hole scores detail his march to glory. (© *Inpho Photography*)

Champagne G-Mac. Graeme McDowell's return to his home town of Portrush led to a series of well-earned celebrations. The US Open trophy — his new best friend — was never far away. (© *Inpho Photography*)

Record breaker. Rory McIlroy didn't just win the 2011 US Open at Congressional Country Club, outside Washington DC. The Ulsterman set record after record in his march to a first Major title, including setting a new low score of 268 strokes for 72 holes in the championship. His putter, much like a magic wand, was irresistible following work with short game guru Dave Stockton. (© *Press Association*)

No backing down. His caddie, J. P. Fitzgerald, took a six-iron out of the bag on the 10th tee of the final round. What Rory McIlroy did with the club was stunning: he hit a towering tee shot on the par 3 to tap-in distance for a birdie. The tee shot was voted 'Shot of the Year' for 2011 on the PGA European Tour. (© *Getty Images*)

Reaching for the sky. The numbers tell the tale: rounds of 65-66-68-69 for 268, 16-under-par, gave Northern Ireland's Rory McIlroy a runaway win by eight shots over runner-up Jason Day of Australia. (© *Inpho Photography*)

The champion returns. Rory McIlroy's home club at Holywood, Co. Down, came out in force to welcome back the 2011 us Open champion. (© *Inpho Photography*)

Chasing destiny. In his 20th appearance in the British Open, Darren Clarke finally found a way to victory at Royal St George's Golf Club, Sandwich. The Northern Irishman — with a swing tailor-made for the windy conditions on the Kent coast — is seen teeing off on the third hole in the final round *en route* to a hugely popular win. (© *Press Association*)

Raising the Claret Jug. All good things come to those who wait, and Darren Clarke's win in the Open at Sandwich — where he finished three strokes clear of Americans Dustin Johnson and Phil Mickelson — finally gave him the opportunity to get his name on the Claret Jug. (© *Press Association*)

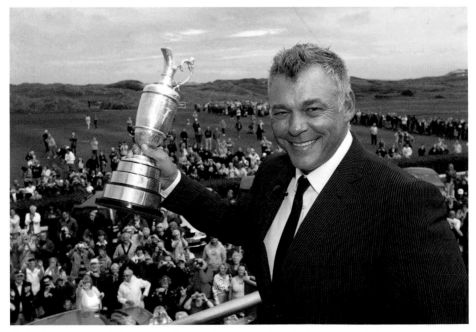

Bringing it home. His win in the 140th Open at Sandwich elevated Darren Clarke to a deserved status as a Major champion. On his homecoming, Clarke gave his gold medal to Royal Portrush Golf Club where it is displayed alongside that of Fred Daly's, winner of the 1947 Open. (© *Inpho Photography*)

Man in control. Rory McIlroy's tee-shot to the par 3 17th hole in his final round of the 2012 US PGA Championship at Kiawah Island, South Carolina, was the product of a player in cruise control on the Ocean Course. The pond between the teeing ground and the green is home to a number of alligators. (© *Getty Images*)

Icing on the cake. What better way to claim your second career Major? Rory McIlroy raises his arms in unison with caddie J. P. Fitzgerald — and the galleries — after he rolls in a birdie putt on the final green to put the icing on the cake in securing the 94th US PGA Championship. (© *Getty Images*)

Mine, all mine! Rory McIlroy poses with the Rodman Wanamaker Trophy after his hugely impressive victory in the 2012 US PGA Championship at Kiawah Island, South Carolina. The Northern Irishman put together a bogey-free finishing round 66 for a tournament total of 275, 13-under-par, to capture his second career Major by a record winning margin of eight strokes. (© *Getty Images*)

extra hard to keep his master patient. 'Kenny was giving me a hard time, trying to keep my head on. This is a tough week and you have to keep your emotions in check. The US Open beats you up a little bit,' conceded McDowell after a round that comprised five birdies and five bogeys that emphasised the up-and-down emotional rollercoaster ride that the links provided.

McDowell had arrived in Pebble Beach on the back of a win in Celtic Manor that was like a birdie fest. G-Mac had, as he put it in that twang that smacked of Ulster with a touch of Alabama, to 'recalibrate the system' for a quite different challenge.

He explained: 'I know my game is in good shape and I was able to come here and prepare well. But it is like a really tough exam. It doesn't matter how much you have studied, it is always going to ask you questions and see if you have the answers. It's such a difficult test you are going to get into position Z at times and I did that on occasions and you have to take your medicine. It is tough not to get frustrated, but sometimes you have got to play your way into these things. On day one, it is extremely important not to shoot your way out of it.'

The smile which accompanied McDowell's words provided an insight into his mindset. He was a happy man. 'I think I am getting more prepared every time I come to a Major. They are difficult, really tough tests of golf, and you just have to enjoy it. I feel like I have learned a lot about the golf course. It doesn't matter how much practice and preparation you do, you really have to get the ball down and get the card in your pocket and see how the golf course is actually playing.'

———

The lie-in, such as it was, lasted until 4.30 am. It was then that Graeme McDowell's alarm call woke him from his slumbers — 'A bit of a rude awakening,' he conceded — for the ride from his Cannery Row hotel to the links at Pebble Beach for the second round of the championship.

For a man given the moniker G-Mac and all of the connotations with speed that such a name suggested, McDowell — competing in his 17th Major championship — moved with considerable stealth as he compiled his score that Friday. He did so fine a job that, when his 68 was added to his opening 71, the 30-year old's midway total of three-under-par 139 was better than anyone else's. He found himself leading the championship.

The symbolism of McDowell's dress sense for his second round wasn't lost on anybody. He was dressed from head to toe in solemn black, as if to show the utmost respect for a links which over the years had induced its fair share of pain on players.

For the second round, the USGA took the decision not to mow the rough. The motor blades didn't touch the grass in the rough for the remainder of the championship, a decision aimed at making the grasses stand more upright. However, as if to prove they had a heart, a decision was also taken to hand-water the greens as corrective action to eradicate bumpiness on the putting surfaces as the rounds progressed.

On a cool day that bore more similarity to his home on the north Antrim coast, McDowell went diligently about his task. Although he had missed the cut in the Masters in April, his season had been transformed by his win in the Wales Open and there was a new confidence about his every move. His second round featured six birdies and three bogeys. The last of those dropped shots came on the ninth, McDowell's finishing hole, which ultimately got fellow-Ulsterman Gareth Maybin inside the cut line under the USGA's 10-shot rule. 'I owe him a pint,' quipped Maybin.

Despite starting his round with a bogey on the 10th, where he found a fairway bunker off the tee, McDowell responded with a birdie on the 11th where he nearly holed out with a gap wedge from 95 yards. A tap-in birdie followed. Another bogey came at the 12th where he was again bunkered, but a 40 footer for birdie on the 14th hole kick-started his round, and further birdies at the 16th and 18th meant he turned in 34 strokes.

McDowell also came back in 34 — on the front nine — with birdies on the fourth, a right-to-left breaking putt from 20 feet, and sixth, from six feet, before finishing with a three-putt bogey on the ninth. 'It's great to be in position going into the weekend. That's what I practise for. I've got two more tough days on this golf course, and I'm just trying to stay disciplined and stay calm and keep doing what I'm doing,' he said.

The steadiness of McDowell was at odds with the performance of others, which included Sergio García and Paul Goydos hitting recovery shots from the seaweed caught on the coastal rocks with the sound of the Pacific waves as an accompaniment.

McDowell's pursuers were a mix of old hands and new guns. Ernie Els, the South African who had twice won the US Open in 1994 and 97, produced some vintage play in matching McDowell's 68 to get into a group of four — alongside Phil Mickelson, the Japanese teenage sensation Ryo Ishikawa and the big-hitting American Dustin Johnson — in a share of second place. The pursuers were two shots adrift of McDowell.

You couldn't keep the smile off Mickelson's face. The five-time runner-up in past US Opens produced the low round of the day, a 66, to add to his opening 75 to leapfrog up the leaderboard. Pádraig Harrington, who got a close-up view of Mickelson's performance, observed: 'Phil didn't miss a shot all day. He was spectacular and I got to see it at first hand. It's certainly the best I've ever seen him play. It was as easy a 66 as you'll ever see.' Harrington had a second successive 73 to trail McDowell by seven shots.

Tiger Woods too was well adrift. He had an adventurous round which included a chip-in birdie on the 11th, his second hole, but also featured a penalty drop on the third where he pulled his drive into horrendous rough down the left of the fairway. Even so, Woods — who shot a 72 for 146 — insisted he liked his position. 'I just need to hole a few more birdies and I will be right there.'

Lee Westwood, who had won the St Jude Classic in Memphis the week beforehand, had a 71 for 145, which had him leaving the course contented. 'It's not a bad position. You can't attack a US Open course. You have to play patient golf and you just have to hang around and not be too aggressive. I feel I can hang around for the next 36 holes and perhaps on Sunday afternoon have a chance. I don't think anybody's going to run away with this.'

One man who knew what it took to win Majors didn't hesitate when asked to consider if G-Mac could follow his footsteps. Pádraig Harrington had a twinkle in his eye as he backed the Ulsterman as a frontrunner. 'Oh, I think Graeme can win,' said Harrington, adding: 'His character is that when he is leading he gets on a run and he is very confident. I honestly think he can win from the front. There are not a lot of people you can say that about, but he is that sort of character.'

McDowell was the man in front at the midway point. Had he allowed himself to dream of winning? 'You know, I'd be lying if I hadn't thought of picking up the trophy on Sunday afternoon. I think that's only natural. But I'm trying to be very realistic about it as well. I'm really trying to put no expectations on myself this weekend because A, I know there's a lot of great players out there, and B, this golf course is extremely difficult. But I'm probably as ready going into the weekend of a Major as I've ever been.

'Is this weekend my weekend? I have no idea. But I'll certainly be giving it my best shot, giving it 100 per cent. If I get a sniff on Sunday afternoon, I'll be ready for it.

'Winning major championships is what I've dreamt of all my life and what I've practised for. That doesn't mean my name is on the trophy. There's a hell of a lot of work to do. This course is ready to bite you any second. I'm going to be relaxed and dis-ciplined and try to keep control of my emotions and see where that leaves me,' said McDowell.

Not everyone was so happy. Rory McIlroy's championship had ended. He hot-tailed it out of California to be back home in Holywood, Co. Down, by the time the defining shots were hit on Sunday.

———

In horse racing, there is a theory about horses for courses. The same philosophy can often by applied to a golfer. A lot of regular tournaments on the PGA Tour and on the European Tour return year after year to the same course and invariably some players contend year after year. It has to do with a course fitting a player's eye, and there was something about Dustin Johnson and Pebble Beach that seemed like a marriage made in heaven.

Johnson had won the past two AT&T National Pro-Ams on the links on the Monterey Peninsula. His booming drives — measuring over 300 yards — meant he could fly over most of the trouble and he also had a propensity, more often than not, to stay on the straight and narrow. It gave him a huge edge on the field.

On a beautifully sunny Saturday, one of those moving days so beloved of player and spectator alike, Johnson laid down his cards. The 6 foot 4 inch American combined distance off the tee with some wonderful approach play and shot a 66 that moved him to five-under-par 207 and put him in pole position to claim a maiden Major title.

Graeme McDowell didn't do too much wrong — eking out a 71 to be three shots adrift of Johnson after 54 holes — but it was the man behind him, Tiger Woods, who grabbed people's attention. Woods, like Johnson, shot a third round 66 that moved him on to the 212 mark, one-under-par. Only three players had reached the three-quarter point of the championship under par.

McDowell and Johnson had been the last two players to be introduced late in the afternoon for the third round. McDowell had been glad to get going. For much of that morning, G-Mac had been killing time. He went for a late breakfast with his dad Kenny and manager Conor Ridge, trawled the internet, went to the Mall and bought an iPad and finally made his way to the course.

By the time the final two players teed off, the roars reverberating around the course were announcing a charge from someone. Not just anyone. It was Woods who was compiling a round that featured eight birdies. The world's No. 1 came home in 31 and settled into a familiar position as clubhouse leader.

On the Monday morning, Woods had played a practice round — as often happened — with Johnson. The two were friendly, and their length off the tee added a dimension to their practice rounds. Johnson, coached by Butch Harmon, had developed into one of the longest hitters on the PGA Tour.

Neither McDowell nor Johnson flinched as word of Woods's endeavours worked its way back. In fact, McDowell started off with back-to-back birdies which increased his lead over Johnson to four strokes. Gradually the pendulum swung to the American with McDowell's driving accuracy — normally one of his strong points — letting him down. The Ulsterman only hit nine fairways in a third round that tested his fortitude.

If there was any inner despondency at losing the advantage to the big-hitting Johnson, it wasn't evident on that Saturday evening. 'To shoot 71 on this layout, not being in control of my game, I'm pretty happy. I felt like I did my job. Three back (going into the final round)? I'm looking forward to it, Sunday in a Major. I'm happy to be in the position I'm in,' said McDowell as he faced into overturning a three-shot deficit. 'Where else would you rather be on a Sunday afternoon but in the last group in a Major at Pebble Beach. Bring it on,' he added.

Johnson had moved into the lead after day three with a wonderful round that ignited with an eagle three on the par 5 fourth hole, where his three-iron approach got a nice kick and ran up to 10 feet. He added further birdies on the sixth and seventh and only stuttered briefly with a bogey on the ninth where he missed a short putt. The momentum continued with a birdie on the 11th before he hit a poor drive on the 13th that led to a bogey. Undeterred, he kept to an aggressive game plan and birdied the 17th and 18th.

'I'm going to be tough to beat. I'm really hitting the ball well right now,' said Johnson in an unaccustomed show of bravado. Moments later he had changed his tune. He was more cautious, more guarded, more realistic. 'I'm going to have to play very well. I'm going to have to putt it good. I'm going to have to hit it good. You can't fake it around this golf course. You just can't do it. You've got to drive it straight. You've got to hit good shots into the greens and you've got to leave yourself uphill putts.'

Johnson headed off to dinner and then to his hotel room to watch television that Saturday evening in unfamiliar territory and with destiny in his own hands. He had a three-shot lead in the US Open, his national championship and one of golf's four Majors. Underneath the façade of coolness, it was only human that the nerves had started to twitch.

———

Daybreak on Sunday welcomed Father's Day, and for Graeme McDowell — who'd first started to play the game as a seven-year old under the guidance of his father Kenny on the rugged Causeway Coast of north Antrim — it seemed right and fitting that his dad was with him on the Monterey Peninsula as he set out in his quest for a first Major title.

He'd slept well, the difference between sleeping with a lead and going to bed as the player chasing a lead.

From the first time McDowell set his eyes on Pebble Beach, he fell in love with the place. As a student at the University of Alabama in 2001, he and his college team mates played a tournament in California but found time to make a pilgrimage of sorts to see for themselves the Pebble Beach Links. 'We were in awe of the place, and thinking, wow. It reminded me of home quite a lot, the coast line and the ocean and just the beauty of it.'

There was no pressure on that visit. He was just a college kid sneaking a peak at the famed landscape. It was the year after Tiger Woods had decimated the field in the 100th US Open, where golf's poster boy had celebrated the centennial hosting of the championship with a performance never before seen in the game. Woods finished up with a 15-stroke winning margin over runners-up Miguel Ángel Jiménez and Ernie Els. It had seemed there were two tournaments that year: one for Woods, and one for everyone else.

McDowell made his way to the course in the knowledge that the 110th US Open remained an open book. Although Johnson held a three-stroke lead and had shown a particular liking for the links in capturing back-to-back AT&T Pebble Beach Pro-Am titles, the USGA traditionally reserved its hardest course set-up for the final round. And McDowell was a player who relished a grind.

When Dustin Johnson, who cut an imposing figure, was introduced to the crowds on the first tee, they reacted as if a coronation of a new champion was a formality. Within three holes, the whole scenario had utterly changed.

Johnson's troubles began with his second shot on the second hole, one of the more nondescript holes on the links as it ran inland away from the ocean. His approach came up short and when Johnson walked up to it, he discovered the ball in a horrible lie in clinging grass on the edge of a bunker. Johnson put both hands on his bent knees as he assessed how he would play the shot, and decided to chip it out left-handed with the club reversed in his hands. The ball moved barely six feet and finished in deep rough. His next shot, his fourth, was an attempted flop shot which moved maybe three feet. By the time Johnson managed to get the ball in the hole, he had run up a triple-bogey seven.

The stunned quiet of the galleries told its own story. It reminded many of the fate that befell Gil Morgan in the 1982 US Open, where he went into the final round with a lead, only to collapse to a closing 81 that allowed Tom Kite to claim the Major.

Johnson's head was reeling as he stood on the third tee box, but his troubles were far from over. Many players used fairway woods off the third tee to position the ball on the fairway over a ravine. Johnson, in his wisdom, opted to use his driver to clear the dogleg. It never got close to finding the fairway. His ball finished somewhere near the 16th green, some 40 yards off line, and his misery was compounded when the ball couldn't be found in the specified time. He made the long walk back to the tee, with a hybrid instead of a driver in his hand, and finished the hole with a double-bogey six. In an ironic twist, Johnson's original ball was found — in the rough but playable — just 19 seconds after the five minute search time had elapsed.

His nightmare continued. On the fourth hole, Johnson blocked his tee shot right. It was last seen going over the cliffs to find a watery grave in the Pacific Ocean. He managed to make a bogey, but his US Open dream was over. In the space of an hour, he covered the first four holes in six-over-par and lost his grip on the tournament.

McDowell had no choice other than to watch Johnson disintegrate in front of his very eyes. As the player paired with Johnson in the final group, he'd watched the carnage unfold. He sought to stay detached. He talked with Kenny, his caddie. He looked away when he could. He got on with his own job.

It was a strange and curious day on the cliff top links. Johnson's meltdown opened the door for those who had started the final round in pursuit. But the usual suspects didn't deliver: Tiger Woods and Ernie Els — who took 40 strokes on his back nine — hit shots over the cliffs, and Phil Mickelson failed to ignite in his bid to add an elusive US Open to his Masters title.

McDowell stepped up to the mark. He followed an opening sequence of four successive pars with a birdie — from 12 feet — on the fifth hole. That birdie was to be the only one he managed in a final round where, as Johnson discovered to his cost, it was more important to grind out scores. Just as the USGA wanted, the championship had turned into a battle for survival. When those hard questions were asked, G-Mac was one man who never flinched.

In the match ahead of McDowell, another player revelled in the tough examination. Frenchman Gregory Havret had gone to the International Qualifying at Walton Heath outside London for the 36-hole tournament which McDowell had bypassed. Havret had failed in three previous attempts to make his way through the qualifying lottery but made it a case of fourth time lucky as he booked his ticket to Pebble Beach.

In truth, Havret had merited barely a notice in the run-up to the championship. His experience of playing in the Majors was very limited and his record was hardly enough to instil fear in other players. Of his four Major appearances, a tied-19th finish at the British Open in Royal Birkdale in 2008 was far and away his best performance. It was the only time he had survived the midway cut. A missed cut at the 2007 British Open and also at the US PGA that same year constituted his only other Major involvement.

Havret, ranked 391st in the world, took a huge step-up in Pebble Beach, where he emerged as the most serious threat to McDowell as other players with bigger names and a host of Majors on their curricula vitae fell by the wayside.

Critically, McDowell — quite literally — had Havret, a good friend, in his sights. Havret was in the penultimate pairing with Woods. McDowell was with Johnson in the final two-ball. Of all the contenders, it was Havret who played the best golf on the back nine — until he reached the par 3 17th hole, where the tee shot was directly towards the Pacific Ocean. Havret found a greenside bunker and failed to get up and down. That bogey put him two shots behind McDowell.

That two-shot lead didn't last long, as McDowell also found a greenside trap and also made bogey. The drama continued to the 18th hole, one of the most picturesque par 5s in the world of golf with the ocean pounding the rocks all the way up the left-hand side. Havret played the finishing hole well and found the green-side bunker in two, splashing out to 10 feet. He had a birdie putt to tie the lead but walked after it as soon as he struck it. He holed a three footer back for par and, typically French, allowed the tears to flow as he felt a closing 72 had come up just short.

Behind him, down the 18th, McDowell — his ball just beyond the famed cypress trees — had been undecided about going for the green in two. He pondered whether to play a two-iron to get close to the green, or to lay up with a five-iron. His caddie Kenny Comboy advised the latter option and G-Mac agreed. He laid up to 99 yards, hit his third shot to 20 feet and two-putted for the championship. He signed for a 74, enough to win by a shot over Havret.

As the sun dipped into a becalmed ocean, the roar of acclaim which greeted McDowell from those crammed in the grandstands and on the hillocks around the 18th green were eerily like those of old. Seismic roars which had once hailed Jack Nicklaus, Tom Watson, Tom Kite and Tiger Woods were now reserved for a 30-year-old Ulsterman, who alone had conquered the toughest examination in Major golf, a player who held the US Open trophy in his hands as if it were too precious to let go.

McDowell, the 110th US Open champion, clutched the trophy and, adopted by the crowd as one of their own, gave them the clichés about filling the cup with Guinness and of how he would never let it down. Just as he had done on the course, where others were spurned in their quest to lay claim to the trophy engraved with famous names, G-Mac wooed them with his charm and his intelligent banter. Yet the twinkle in his eye was a recognition that he, more than anyone, knew that this was his destiny.

Close by, his father Kenny — who had introduced him to the sport as a young boy — stood at the back of the 18th green, sunglasses on to hide the tears in his eyes as much as to block out the low setting sun. He shook his head, almost as if he couldn't understand what his son had just done. Shortly after McDowell had rolled in the short par putt on the 72nd hole, his 284th stroke of a championship which had left carnage and chaos for other contenders, Kenny ran on to the green to embrace his son.

'Happy Father's Day,' whispered McDowell.

'You're some kid,' replied the dad.

————

Graeme McDowell's world had changed. He held the beautiful trophy in his hands and looked at the names engraved on it and, in particular, those who had worked their magic on the Pebble Beach Links: Jack Nicklaus, Tom Watson, Tom Kite, Tiger Woods, Graeme McDowell.

He had worked hard to achieve his dream, and had taken some tough decisions. He had changed clubs, caddies, coaches, management companies and moved home to Portrush — close to his parents Kenny and Marian and brothers George and Gary — to regain perspective. He still kept a house in Lake Nona in Florida, but Portrush was home.

Comboy had teamed up with McDowell four years previously. When player and bagman started out, Comboy honestly admitted that he didn't see a future Major champion. Not then. But the player made progressive and vast improvements. According to Comboy: 'You could never fault his attitude, his potential to improve or his work ethic.'

Conor Ridge also saw that deep-rooted desire. McDowell had been part of an International Sports Management stable full of thoroughbreds which looked after Lee Westwood, Ernie Els, Rory McIlroy, Louis Oosthuizen, Charl Schwartzel and many others.

McDowell made the decision at the end of 2007 to move to fresh pastures and sought out Ridge's Horizon Sports Management based in Dublin.

'We were shaping ourselves up to attract some pretty big players and you need someone to buy into your vision for what you are trying to do,' explained Ridge.

'Graeme spoke about getting a lot of energy from a new group of people around him, and maybe a company being built around him which is exactly what is happening. It was a big move for him. He's left one of the biggest companies in the world and gone to a smaller one and I suppose he was buying into me to a certain degree.'

Every move which McDowell had made, turned out to be a winning one! The proof of the pudding, as it were, was in his hands on the 18th green at Pebble Beach on that Sunday evening as he shouted out a special wish to his mother Marian, who had watched her son's moment of triumph on television. She was in Spain.

———

Graeme McDowell was pulled from Billy to Jack on a Sunday evening that dragged into the night and then into the early morning. The media demands — of print, radio and TV — took an age, and eventually he and his entourage made it to Foley's Irish Bar in Carmel, where a proper party celebrated the sport's newest Major champion.

G-Mac doesn't know for sure what time he made it back to his plush five-star hotel on the seafront in Cannery Row. It was late, or early, depending on whether time is judged by night or morning. When he woke at an unearthly hour of the morning with barely any sleep, he felt the need to check that it wasn't a dream. The sight of the us Open trophy beside his bed allayed any fears.

With a spectacular view out on to the Pacific, what was a guy to do? Why, blast music and play air guitar of course! McDowell didn't care if anyone listening thought a madman had checked into the hotel.

On Monday morning, McDowell left his luxury hotel with the trophy tucked under his arm. He was stopped by well-wishers as he made the short walk to Peet's Coffee & Tea House where John Steinbeck novels lined the bookshelves. Over the past week he had whiled away many an hour in the coffee house. He said his goodbyes to the staff who had adopted this Irishman far from home as one of their own.

McDowell's lack of sleep didn't dim his senses, as he articulately appraised the journey he had taken to become a Major champion. 'This game, when you are in the wilderness, can be a bleak and dark place. The tough times are tough. The game gives you no love back. When you want love, it doesn't give you it. When you hope something is going to happen, it never happens. The second you start believing in yourself and you let it happen, it is amazing what's around the corner.

'I keep saying the win in the Wales Open (two weeks previously) was very significant because it was a different win. It felt different. It didn't feel like Scotland. It didn't feel like Sweden. It didn't feel like Italy or Korea. It felt very right and it felt, right, let's go. It felt like it kick-started my summer, but I didn't know what was around the corner.

'Did I think I was going to win a Major championship? No. But it felt like I was on the verge of a big summer . . . I'm a motivated guy, a driven guy, and I have people around me that drive me towards my goals. I knew if I had a chance to contend that I was going to be ready. I wish I could bottle up the way I felt.'

——

His new life as a Major champion — as the US Open champion — saw Graeme McDowell embraced by the Americans. On that Monday, 21 June, the day after his breakthrough Major win, two of television's biggest names vied for him. David Letterman wanted him. So too Jay Leno. McDowell decided to go on *The Tonight Show* with Jay Leno and shared a studio with the actress Dakota Fanning and the singer Crystal Bowersox. He was in the big time.

How did G-Mac get to Los Angeles? By private jet, of course. Marquis Jets, one of his sponsors, put a jet at his disposal. McDowell's win at Pebble Beach had moved him on to a new level and, if the interview on the Leno show gave an insight into another world, it got even better later that evening. His hotel was in Beverly Hills and, as it happened, his favourite TV series — *Entourage* — were in the middle of filming when they heard G-Mac was near by. He was invited on to the set to partake in a cameo role.

That his scene, where he bumped into fictional sports agent Ari Gold — played by Jeremy Piven — on the way into the toilet, never saw the light of day on *Entourage*, a casualty of the cutting room floor, didn't matter.

McDowell had arrived.

Chapter 7 ∾

HOLYWOOD STAR WRITES RECORD-BREAKING SCRIPT

111th US Open Championship, Congressional
Country Club, Bethesda, Maryland, USA

June 2011

To the outside world, it was often hard to see how any professional golfer could garner any true perspective. They were a pampered lot. Many flew in private jets, either owned by the player himself or hired by the hour from NetJets or Marquis Jets. All enjoyed *haute cuisine* at whichever tournament they decided was worthy of their presence. They were festooned with clothing — cashmere sweaters, stylish trousers, rain gear and golf balls, and the most technological up-to-date golf clubs that research and money can produce. Courtesy cars were *de rigueur*. It was a good and often great life.

How did any professional golfer get true perspective?

In the week before the 111th US Open at Congressional Country Club in Bethesda, Maryland — not a million miles from the White House in downtown Washington DC — Rory McIlroy, in his role as a sporting ambassador with UNICEF Ireland, found perspective. He visited the Caribbean country of Haiti which, 18 months on from a devastating earthquake, still strove to recover from its effects and struggled to find any normalcy for its people.

McIlroy helped distribute cholera prevention supplies. He visited children in a displacement camp. He held them in his arms. He visited makeshift schools. He taught them how to wash.

'I remember driving past the Presidential palace and the dome on the top was just hanging off. I was just thinking to myself, if they can't even repair the palace, then they can't do anything. They just need so much help.

McIlroy was accompanied on the two-day humanitarian visit by UNICEF representative in Haiti Françoise Gruloos-Ackermans who remarked of the golfer's visit: 'Visits by McIlroy and other humanitarian supporters bring attention to these needs and high-light the work that UNICEF and its partners are doing to address this and help children in Haiti realise their rights to education, protection and health care.'

For McIlroy, the experience was an eye-opening one. 'It's definitely not nice to see. It gives you a huge sense of being so fortunate and just doing normal things every day. Even having street lights and having smooth roads, you think those things are just a given. But those people (in Haiti) don't have that, and they might not have that for the next 15 or 20 years.'

He had perspective.

McIlroy was asked if any of the children in Haiti actually knew who he was.

'None of them,' answered McIlroy.

Perspective.

———

Two months previously, on Sunday 10 April 2011, Rory McIlroy set out in the final round of the US Masters, destined to be champion. On the Saturday he had rolled in a 30-foot birdie putt on the 17th hole that prompted the sort of roar normally reserved for Tiger Woods or Phil Mickelson, and the next day he took a four-stroke lead into the closing 18 holes. It was the biggest 54-hole lead since Woods had led by nine in his maiden Major win in 1997.

McIlroy failed to close the deal. From a man with destiny in his own hands when teeing off at the first, he metamorphosed into someone who could do nothing right. One shot after another, it seemed, went astray. It was the hardest and cruellest lesson that anyone had been taught around the pristine Augusta National course for a long, long time.

There were echoes of Greg Norman's collapse in 1996 when he saw a six-shot 54-hole lead evaporate as Nick Faldo took the title. But McIlroy was younger, seemingly more innocent.

On that Sunday it all went horribly wrong for golf's next coming star. The meltdown started on the 10th hole, known as Camellia and named after a flower found mostly in Asian climes. Apparently it possessed soothing fragrances. That day, Camellia provided nothing but angst for McIlroy. The downhill par 4 of 495 yards — traditionally the hole ranked toughest on the manicured Augusta National layout — required the player to turn the ball right-to-left off an elevated tee around a corner lined with towering cathedral pines.

McIlroy's woes started with a drive which crashed into a tree limb barely 100 yards in front of him and ricocheted so far left that it came to rest between two cabins, known as Peek and Berckmans. The player had no option other than to chip back towards the fairway. The trouble continued when his third shot was pulled left of the green. His fourth shot clipped a tree branch. When he finally got the ball into the hole, it was for a triple-bogey seven.

The heartache continued as McIlroy entered 'Amen Corner' — that sequence of holes from the 11th to the 13th — and stayed with him until he exited. On the 11th hole, he safely reached the putting surface in two strokes, but then took three putts for a bogey. On the par 3 12th, he again safely found the green with his tee shot, but then four-putted from 15 feet for a double-bogey five. When he put his drive into Rae's Creek off the 13th tee, he looked like a lost boy.

It would have been easy for McIlroy to slip away after he exited the recorder's tent at the back of the 18th green that Sunday evening in Augusta, where South African Charl Schwartzel was hailed as the champion of the 75th Masters. It said much for McIlroy's character that he hung around. He faced the music and he blamed nobody but himself. He was gracious and patient. He promised he would return stronger for the experience.

Nobody believed him.

As Norman, who had suffered a much-documented collapse of his own in the 1996 US Masters when Faldo benefited from his demise, remarked afterwards: 'I know exactly how he felt. What is it with golf destiny? Isn't it strange? It taps you on the back of the head and it either pushes you ahead or it pushes you back. Who determines that? It's crazy.'

———

The view from the grandiose clubhouse at Congressional Country Club — in a part of the world where there are more movers and shakers, certainly in politics, than anywhere on the planet — was of hilly, tree-lined terrain called the Blue Course which, in the 111th US Open, was charged with asking the sternest questions of the season.

The course was 7,574 yards long to a par of 71 and had greens that ran up to 14.5 on the stimpmeter, the device used to gauge the speed of a ball on the putting surface.

Congressional — on the outskirts of the US capital — didn't hide its exclusivity. Anyone with desires on joining had to respect a waiting period of up to eight years, if they were lucky, and a number of US Presidents — William Howard Taft, Woodrow Wilson, Warren Harding, Calvin Coolidge, Herbert Hoover, Dwight Eisenhower and Gerald Ford — had been members in their time.

Originally built in the 1920s as 'an informal common ground where politicians and businessmen could meet as peers, unconstrained by red tape', the course — designed by Devereux Emmet, redesigned by Robert Trent Jones in the 1950s and given a modern makeover by his son Rees Jones for the third staging of the US Open — was visually stunning.

Graeme McDowell, the defending champion, observed: 'Aesthetically it's beautiful, real old school. Great trees, great definition, really well bunkered, great greens.'

The club had survived the Second World War by leasing its property as training grounds for the super-secret Office of Strategic Services. In 1955 the club offered to play host to the US Open but was told in no uncertain terms that it lacked the demands of being a genuine championship test, and so Robert Trent Jones was engaged to make it one. Among the changes he made was to combine a par 4 and a par 3 hole to make a gargantuan par 5, the 636-yard ninth hole.

Significant changes were made to the Blue Course for the 2011 championship compared to 1997 when Ernie Els triumphed in the final round over Tom Lehman and Colin Montgomerie. At 7,574 yards, it became one of the longest in US Open history — only Torrey Pines in 2008 was longer — and all 18 green complexes were rebuilt.

Many of the alterations which Rees Jones made for the 111th US Open were ones, he insisted, that his father would have made if more money and better equipment had been available to him half a century earlier. 'My father's approach to preparing a course for an (US) Open was to preserve par, to keep the winning score around or above par . . . My approach is much different. I try to make the course play fair, to give everyone more options as well as more challenges . . . The best golf will most often win. You don't have a fluke winner.'

The decision to rebuild all 18 greens was actually taken by the Congressional Club to improve drainage and to get rid of the perceived troublesome poa annua greens which traditionally suffered in the summer heat. The new greens were a hybrid bentgrass with a deeper root structure. The green staff used GPS technology to replicate the old contours.

Those players who teed up in the US Open faced a tough examination. Nobody could have foreseen how Rory McIlroy took the USGA's test.

———

Tiger Woods had hosted his own tournament at Congressional — the AT&T National — for a number of years on the regular PGA Tour. He had even won it once, in 2009, and there was a sense that the USGA had perhaps given the former world No. 1 an advantage by returning the course to the US Open roster. Except for one thing: Woods never made it to the 111th US Open.

Woods suffered a sprain to his left knee and a strain to his left Achilles tendon in the third round of the Masters in April. He had been wearing a protective boot in the hope of regaining fitness for the US Open, but a week before the tournament he withdrew on medical advice.

————

With no Tiger Woods in the field, the hopes of America — again — were placed on the shoulders of Phil Mickelson. Year after year, Mickelson went into the US Open with a swagger and left with a shuffle. It just never went his way. Some years others got in his way; other years he contrived to get in his own way. A classic case in point was his tee shot on the 18th hole of the final round of the 2006 US Open championship at Winged Foot. 'I'm such an idiot,' Mickelson, in a state of shock, remarked afterwards. Geoff Ogilvy strutted away with the trophy.

In fact, nobody had tasted the sourness of defeat in the US Open more frequently than Mickelson. On five occasions, more often than not with the title within his grasp, Lefty had walked away as a runner-up: to Payne Stewart at Pinehurst in 1999; to Tiger Woods at Bethpage in 2002; to Retief Goosen at Shinnecock

Hills in 2004; to Ogilvy in 2006; and to Lucas Glover at Bethpage in 2009.

Mickelson was gung-ho in the days before the tournament at Congressional. As he put it, 'I've come close five times now . . . which is actually a good sign in the sense that it's on a course set-up that probably nobody thought I would do well on throughout my career. And yet I've played some of my better golf in the US Open. I just need a few breaks here and there, or maybe a few less mistakes here or there, to be able to come out on top. I believe that I'm playing some good golf. Ball-striking wise, I think it's the best it's been in the last three, four or five months.'

Mickelson professed to be up to the challenge. When it came time for him to hit his first tee shot of the championship, those around the 10th tee box — his starting hole — cringed in disbelief. His first shot in his quest for a coveted US Open was under-hit and came up short in the lake which guarded the green. He opened with a double-bogey five. The golfing gods had let him know his fate early.

———

Rory McIlroy's first round had none of Phil Mickelson's flaws, or anybody else's for that matter. On that Thursday, the Ulsterman — who had turned 22 years of age just the previous month, in May — was utterly flawless. He hit 17 of 18 greens in regulation and opened his quest for a maiden Major with a 65, six-under-par. It gave him a three-shot lead.

On a day that had opened with grey cloud cover and some soft rain, the course — trimmed back to 7,514 yards by the USGA, just 60 yards short of its maximum — provided a tough examination for many. South Korea's Y.E. Yang, the USPGA champion of 2009, showed that a score was possible as he covered the homeward nine holes in 33 shots as he signed for a 68. It proved to be an appetiser for the main course served by McIlroy.

If anyone expected McIlroy's first round in a Major since his much-publicised Masters meltdown to be any way traumatic, they were to be proved wrong. His round was, quite simply, breath-taking. He started on the 10th tee alongside Mickelson — who celebrated his 41st birthday — and Dustin Johnson and, while the two Americans zigzagged their way around the course, the young pretender took a mere 32 strokes to the turn.

McIlroy looked a different man to the one who had capitu-lated on that final Sunday at the Masters. His ball-striking was near perfect, his putting — having started to work with short game guru Dave Stockton on that aspect of his game after Augusta — was pure. On the turn for home, he birdied the first and rolled in a tap-in from 18 inches for another birdie on the fourth. On the par 5 sixth, a hole which played to 575 yards, McIlroy hit a drive of 320 yards to 12 feet and two-putted for his final birdie of a round that had the galleries adopting him as a favoured son.

Only once did McIlroy veer away from perfection. On the 14th hole, his fifth of the day, he hit an approach into a greenside bunker and played an average recovery to 15 feet. The putter came to his rescue as he sank the putt on the slick green for a par.

When his day's work was done, McIlroy was asked if the way-wardness of Mickelson and Johnson had distracted him. He seemed surprised at the question. 'No, no,' he replied, 'I don't think it affects you at all. All you're trying to concentrate on is your own game. It's a Major championship, and the toughest championship of them all is the US Open. You can't let any other thought get in your head. You're just trying to concentrate entirely on your game and trying to get that ball around the course in as few strokes as possible.'

What McIlroy had done was show the world that there were no residual wounds left over from his travails at Augusta. 'I don't know if it says that I've just got a short memory. I don't know. I took the experience from Augusta and I learned a lot from it . . . but I feel like these good starts in the Majors are very much down to my preparations.'

McIlroy took the first round by the scruff of the neck. But Graeme McDowell, the defending champion, took up the challenge. The task of defending a Major championship title, as everyone knew, was extremely difficult. Pádraig Harrington had successfully defended the British Open in 2008 just two years after Tiger Woods had successfully gone back to back in 2006. But the US Open, for some reason, was different. Not since Curtis Strange, in 1989, had any player successfully retained the trophy.

The famed silver trophy with the winged lady atop had been handed back to the USGA by McDowell, but his first round endeavours — a commendable 70 — indicated a hankering for its return to him.

McDowell started his round with a bogey. 'Sometimes that can be the slap in the face you need on a Thursday morning,' he remarked philosophically. But he didn't drop another shot in a composed round and responded immediately to that opening hole setback with a birdie on the par 3 second where he hit a rescue club to six feet. He then added another birdie on the sixth, and almost Faldoesque, reeled off 12 successive pars.

'I set myself the challenge to go out and be patient, to stick to my processes. I have been a bit too focused on results lately and I knew I had to get back to basics, to think properly and to get back into my good routines … It felt normal out there, just like another Major championship and it didn't feel like I was the defending champion. I executed my game plan and felt good doing it. It's an old cliché, that you can't win a tournament on a Thursday, but you can play yourself out of it,' remarked McDowell.

On a day where the top three players were grouped together, they failed to fire on all cylinders: world No. 1 Luke Donald opened with a 75, having had a blistering birdie-birdie start to his round, while Lee Westwood and Martin Kaymer each registered 74s. 'None of us played well. I think we all just about got what we deserved,' remarked Westwood.

———

On the Friday morning of the second round of the 111th US Open, half an hour before his scheduled tee time, Rory McIlroy exhibited what would be a rare moment of human frailty at Congressional Country Club. It had nothing to do with a wayward drive or a plugged lie in a bunker. It had nothing to do with a downhill putt on lightning-fast greens. McIlroy's problem was that he couldn't find his ball marker.

Stuart Cage, from the International Sports Management group who managed his affairs at the time, searched his own pockets but only found paper notes rather than nickels or cents.

But he solved the problem by approaching a couple of nearby television reporters who willingly proffered coins to pass on to the golfer. It was an anxious preamble to what turned out to be a quite remarkable day for McIlroy.

With his pre-round routine completed, his array of shots on the driving range followed by some putting on the practice green, McIlroy joined Phil Mickelson and Dustin Johnson on the first tee. There was no discernible difference in the shouts from the galleries to each player.

'Go Phil!'

'Go Dustin!'

'Go Rory!'

As the warm morning developed into a hot day, those roars from behind the ropes were increasingly for one man, the one who wasn't American.

For a stretch on the front nine, it seemed as if Johnson — who had seemed destined to win the US Open the previous year at Pebble Beach, only to suffer a final round collapse that opened the door for Graeme McDowell to walk through — wanted to simply slink back into the shadows. Johnson, tall and athletic, couldn't hide and he couldn't stay in the slipstream of his playing partners as McIlroy and Mickelson went on a birdie blitz on the front nine.

'Go Phil!' shouted two elderly men, who perhaps should have known better, to Mickelson as he trooped off the seventh tee. Lefty had just grabbed his second successive birdie on the sixth and responded to the balding fans with a subtle turn of the head. It was a gesture sufficient to send the pair delirious, in the way that only sports fans who earn even the briefest of acknowledgments from their idol can do.

'You got the nod from Phil,' one shouted at the other, followed by the obligatory high fives as hands smacked against hands. Perhaps they should have looked for the nod from McIlroy, for it was to be his day more than anyone's.

Apart from failing to locate his chosen ball marker before the round, almost everything McIlroy did on that Friday was faultless. The eighth hole, a par 4 of 350 yards and seen as something of a respite for players amidst a series of long holes, provided McIlroy with one of those moments where players believed fate was calling. McIlroy played an iron off the tee and, left with 114 yards to the flag, hit a half-shot wedge approach. From the moment he made contact, he knew it was good. He kept his pose. The ball pitched 30 feet past the hole and spun back into the cup for an eagle two.

There was no nod, but there was a grin from Mickelson who then broke into a round of applause. McIlroy too grinned and shook his head and then did a little fist pump with his caddie J. P. Fitzgerald. He shook his head again, and then regained his composure as he walked on to the green and took the applause from those crowded around the putting surface. McIlroy had started the day at six-under-par following his opening round 65. His birdies at the fourth and sixth holes and the eagle on the eighth had moved him to 10-under. He was running away from the field.

McIlroy, far removed from the player who looked so lost on the final day of the Masters just two months previously, stayed cool and calm.

On the 10th tee, as McIlroy stood in the shade of a parasol and looked down towards the green where Steve Stricker, David Toms and Retief Goosen were holing out, someone in the mass of people around the clubhouse shouted to the Ulsterman.

'Ease up on them, Rory,' came the call, to some amusement from those around him.

McIlroy had no intention of taking his foot off the pedal. He was in the mood for more birdies. He negotiated his way safely through the tough run of holes from the 10th to the 13th and then claimed another birdie on the par 4 14th hole where he hit a six-iron approach from 190 yards to six feet and rolled in the putt.

As McIlroy, Johnson and Mickleson walked to the 15th tee, the enormity of what was unfolding hit Mickelson. 'We're not going to be worrying about the 10-shot rule,' said Mickelson, a reference to the USGA rule than anyone within that margin of the 36-hole leader would make the weekend cut. Instead, the other rule — that the top-60 and ties would survive into the final two rounds — was in vogue. McIlroy was putting quite a distance between himself and the field.

On that day, nobody wanted McIlroy's masterclass to end. After hitting his four-iron approach to the par 5 16th to set up another eagle opportunity, Fitzgerald, his faithful caddie, turned and said: 'I didn't think I would see a shot better than the one to the 14th. But that was even better.' Unfortunately for him, McIlroy didn't convert the 10-foot eagle putt. But he tapped in for a birdie that was followed by another birdie from 15 feet on the 17th which created another piece of US Open history: he became the first ever player in its storied history to reach 13-under-par in the championship.

'The game's easy when you hit it straight and make every putt. It's a wonderful game,' observed Mickelson afterwards. 'No course is too tough when you hit it like that. Rory played terrific. It was fun to watch, although I (tried not) to see too much of it.'

As if to demonstrate some human frailty, McIlroy's play of the 18th was the only mistake he made in almost six hours on the golf course. Mickelson had just put his own approach into the lake guarding the green when McIlroy hit his approach. He sought to turn the ball around the trees towards the front of the green, but got too much movement and watched as his ball too found a watery grave. It led to a double-bogey six.

McIlroy retrieved the ball from the hole and back-handed the Titleist into the lake behind the 18th green, then bounced across the pontoon bridge with all the grace of someone with the ability to walk on water. He had a strut in his step, and deserved to have an air of superiority. He signed for a second round 66 for a midway total of 131, 11-under-par. It gave him a record low 36-hole total in the history of the US Open and allowed him to establish a six-stroke lead over the second placed player, Y.E. Yang of South Korea.

The double-bogey was a blip, nothing more. McIlroy described the attempted recovery shot from the trees on the 18th hole: 'The club turned over a bit. He went on, 'I'm very happy with my position. I couldn't have asked for any more standing on the first tee. If I keep playing the way I'm playing, I've got a good chance.'

Rory McIlroy's performances over the opening two rounds were among the greatest in the history of the championship. In compiling the lowest 36-hole aggregate in US Open history —

breaking by one the mark set by American Ricky Barnes at Bethpage Black in 2009 — McIlroy had taken huge strides in his quest for a first career Major title.

Yet the golfer from Holywood seemed less in awe of the achievement than just about anybody. His feet remained firmly on the ground. 'You know, it's funny to me, (but) it seems quite simple. I'm hitting fairways. I'm hitting greens. I'm holing my fair share of putts and that's really been the key . . . I've just stuck to my game plan and committed to my targets.'

McIlroy's modest assessment of his own game was at odds with the problems experienced by the majority of the field. Only 14 players managed to reach the halfway stage with sub-par totals. Those in pursuit seemed more beguiled with McIlroy's play than the player himself.

It seemed for all the world that the learning experience of his collapse at Augusta had changed him. What's more, McIlroy had demonstrated an old head on young shoulders by seeking out the counsel of Jack Nicklaus. Two weeks prior to the US Open, McIlroy had a talk with Nicklaus at the Memorial tournament in Dublin, Ohio, which the 18-time Major champion hosted annually on the PGA Tour.

Of that talk with Nicklaus, a man half a century older, McIlroy revealed: 'Jack said he always put pressure on himself, that he expected to play well. He expected to be up there all the time. And he said to me, "I expect you to do the same thing." I took a lot from it, (that) you've got to go out there with a belief you're playing well and to put yourself in position to win.'

McIlroy added: 'After Augusta, I said I needed to be a little more cocky, a little more arrogant on the golf course, and to think a little bit more about myself, which I've tried to incorporate a little bit, just on the golf course. I just try and have a bit of an attitude, you know.'

The new cocky attitude mixed well with McIlroy's meticulous preparation. In the three Major championships prior to the US Open at Congressional, McIlroy had been in the frame to win: he finished third behind South African Louis Oosthuizen in the British Open at St Andrews in 2010, third behind Germany's Martin Kaymer in the 2010 US PGA Championship at Whistling Straits, and he held the 54-hole lead at the Masters, only to capitulate in the final round. The closest call had actually come in the PGA, where he finished just one shot outside of a play-off that involved Kaymer and Bubba Watson.

McIlroy planned his attack on the 111th US Open even more meticulously. He had visited Congressional for two days prior to going to Haiti and run over the course with his caddie Fitzgerald. The two men paid particular attention to the greens and mapped out the contours. The idea was also to get the line off the tee and on the intended approaches into the greens.

Every possible box was ticked, and McIlroy had departed for Haiti convinced that the course set-up was to his liking. The proof of the pudding came with his opening 65 that was followed by a 66 that was arguably the better round of the two, despite the one shot differential in the score.

McIlroy's second round featured five birdies, an eagle and a double-bogey on the 18th. His play from tee to green was clinical: he found 15 of 18 greens in regulation and, once on those greens, the work he'd done with former US Ryder Cup captain Dave Stockton Snr was clear for all to see.

The tie-up with Stockton had come about after his Masters mishap in April. The McIlroy-Stockton work had as much to do with a green-reading routine rather than any new technique. 'People often said to me, we think you're too quick on the greens. But Dave thought the opposite. "You're taking too much time. Why are you taking three practice strokes? Don't take any practice strokes any more." I see the target, where I want to hit it and just go with it. If I have any sort of technical thing in my thoughts, in my stroke, it would just be to keep the back of my left hand going towards the target.'

For putt after putt after putt, McIlroy's rhythm worked beautifully.

———

A weather delay of some 42 minutes later on the Friday afternoon — allied with slow play — meant that 12 players never got to finish their second rounds and were forced to return to the course the following day. Rory McIlroy had long finished before such weather interruptions and his plans for the Friday night included watching the movie *Hangover II*, a comedy he felt would have him in the right frame of mind for the main part of the examination and possible redemption for his Masters meltdown, which actually seemed to be more a preoccupation for the media than for the player.

'It's been two very, very good days of golf and I have put myself in a great position. But I know more than probably anybody else what can happen,' said McIlroy. He was referring to his final round collapse in the Masters where he closed with a nightmarish

80 that saw him not only relinquish a four-stroke 54-hole lead but tumble down the leaderboard to ultimately finish in 15th position. 'So,' he added, 'I've got to stay really focused and try and finish this thing off.'

Maybe it was because McIlroy's Masters travails were so fresh in the memory. Maybe it was because professional golfers have eternal hope. Maybe it was because the course was expected to firm up as the championship reached its critical stage. But, on that Friday night at Congressional, few players were willing to throw in the towel.

Sure, there was an acceptance of McIlroy's brilliance over the first two rounds. As Brandt Snedeker, one of the emerging new generation of Americans, put it: 'I think everybody would agree Rory's probably got more talent in his pinky (little finger) than I have in my whole body. He is unbelievably talented, shooting those kind of numbers and swinging the golf club the way he does. I love watching him play because it's a very classical, beautiful golf swing.'

Snedeker reached the halfway point as part of a quintet of players tied in third place, all of nine shots behind McIlroy. The other members of the group were Sergio García, Robert Garrigus, Matt Kuchar and former Masters champion Zach Johnson.

García seemed to have much on his mind, despite being part of the chasing pack — albeit a distant one — as they headed into the weekend. 'If you're hitting it all over the shop, it's quite difficult to give yourself chances. You're fighting to make pars. I have bigger worries than Rory McIlroy,' observed the Spaniard.

Rory McIlroy slept on a six-shot lead on Friday night and woke up at eight o'clock on Saturday morning with a hell of a lot of time left to kill. One of the problems faced by any 36-hole leader in any of the Majors concerned the art of killing time, as they were traditionally handed a late afternoon tee time in the final pairing.

On Saturday morning, McIlroy, the player, had arranged to meet McIlroy, the father, for breakfast at 9.30. Rory spent an hour and a half in bed and made a couple of phone calls to friends back home in Northern Ireland before he joined his dad, Gerry.

McIlroy's father hadn't gone to the Masters in April and instead watched on television at home. The face-to-face father-son chats were missing in Augusta, and over breakfast that Saturday morning the two talked of what was likely to happen in the third round and how he was going to play. Gerry, a very good amateur who had introduced his son to the game almost as soon as he had learned to walk, kept reassuring him. 'You played great the last couple of days. There's no reason why it's going to be any different today. Just go out and do your thing.'

After breakfast there was still a lot of time to kill. McIlroy returned to his room and watched a movie on his laptop and made another few phone calls home to friends. He was in no rush. A weather delay meant that his tee time had been pushed back further, to after four o'clock in the afternoon.

The conditions that Saturday were again favourable to scoring and, on what was known in the trade as 'moving day', a number of players did indeed make their move. One of them was Australian Jason Day, who had finished runner-up to Charl Schwartzel in the Masters. Day shot a third round 65 to finish on five-under-par. England's Lee Westwood, who also shot a 65, joined him.

McIlroy wasn't to be shifted, however. The Ulsterman didn't quite match the brilliance of his 65 in the first round or the 66 in the second. He shot a third round 68 that left him on a total of 199, 14-under-par.

When the numbers were crunched on the Saturday evening, McIlroy held an eight-stroke lead over the persistent Y.E. Yang, in second place, and continued to add his name to the us Open record book: his three-day total of 199 bested by one stroke the mark set in 2003 by Jim Furyk, the winner that year at Olympia Fields outside Chicago.

McIlroy admitted he felt some nervous pressure as he set off on his third round, but an up-and-down par save from 90 yards on the third hole seemed to galvanise him. He relaxed, and helped in no small way by the support from the galleries who had adopted him as one of their own, he found his rhythm.

The show of support from the American galleries on that Saturday was spine-tingling. At one point in the afternoon, as roars of 'Let's go R-O-R-EE' reverberated around the course, American Zach Johnson stood in the middle of the 14th fairway like a statue. He appeared frozen, unable to move as the shouts from the adjacent 12th fairway directed towards McIlroy had a hypnotic effect on him.

Johnson's veteran caddie, a man by the name of Damon Green, eventually had enough. A former tour player who had taken on the task of caddying to stay in the heart of the game, Green probably thought he had seen and heard everything in his golfing life. He turned to the crowds and yelled to them to be quiet. He got only a temporary respite.

Not long after, the chant started again and grew louder and louder. In the absence of Tiger Woods, a new kind of mania had been born. The American crowds had embraced McIlroy. Rory-mania was born. And as McIlroy went about his business, he was met by a standing ovation as he approached each and every green.

The danger which McIlroy faced as he headed into the third round with a six-stroke advantage over Yang was that his game plan would change, or that he would become more conservative. To counteract any such possibilities, McIlroy gave himself a number of targets. The big one was to reach 15-under-par for the championship. He didn't manage to achieve that one, but the other 'little goals', as he called them, were met. These were strategies to play a three-hole stretch in one-under or level par, to break the round into segments so that he avoided getting ahead of himself.

McIlroy kept to his task admirably, and his third successive round in the 60s meant he increased his lead from six to eight strokes. It didn't always come easily. He made important par saves on the third and fourth holes and, after he made bogey on the 10th, where his seven-iron tee shot found a rear greenside bunker, he bounced back with a birdie on the 11th hole.

The year previously, McIlroy had gone into the 110th US Open at Pebble Beach with a pep in his step on the back of a maiden US Tour win in the Quail Hollow Championship. He had exited the Major before the third round and was back home outside Belfast to watch on television as his friend Graeme McDowell claimed a Major breakthrough.

Twelve months on, McIlroy was a different player. He had led for three rounds of the Masters — only to lose the lead in the crucial final round — and had bounced back to lead for the first three rounds of the US Open at Congressional. As he put it, 'I've changed immensely. You need to mature as a golfer, and all these experiences that I've had since that point (missing the cut at Pebble Beach) last year have helped me a lot. I've learned a lot about myself and a lot about my game. I'm definitely thinking a lot better out on the golf course, making better decisions.'

———

When Rory McIlroy — dressed in a blue shirt for the fourth straight day, a decision taken by Oakley, one of his sponsors — arrived at his locker for the final round of the US Open, he found a message written on notepaper from Graeme McDowell. 'What golf course are you playing?' asked the US Open champion of 2010. The note then urged him to keep going as he had done for the first three rounds.

By the time McIlroy got to the first tee, his then manager Andrew 'Chubby' Chandler — who had just seen off another of his stable, Lee Westwood, in the penultimate pairing — was there to send off his man.

After his third round 65 on Saturday, Westwood had stubbornly refused to concede that McIlroy was out of sight. 'You don't know how Rory is going to do. You don't know how he's going to deal with a big lead. He had a big lead at the Masters and didn't deal with it well. There's pressure on him with regards to that, so we'll see. All I can do is control my game and try and shoot as low a score as possible.'

Chandler, a former tour pro who set up the International Sports Management agency on his retirement from playing, was a larger than life figure who had enjoyed a spectacular run of success in the crossover from the 2010 season into 2011. One of his players, Louis Oosthuizen, had literally run away with the 2010 British Open at St Andrews, and then another South African, Charl Schwartzel, had come through at the Masters.

'I don't think there'll be anyone on the streets of Belfast or Dublin or anywhere,' quipped Chandler.

For that matter, on that Sunday afternoon, it looked as if the streets of Washington DC had been cleared and everyone had descended on Congressional Country Club — some 10 miles north of the White House — for the final round. The galleries were lined 10 deep on either side of the fairway all the way down the first fairway. All eyes were on one man.

McIlroy looked confident and assured as he limbered up on the first tee. His caddie J. P. Fitzgerald took out the old three-wood — a favoured club with a slight scratch on the clubhead — which had been put into the bag for the week. McIlroy's first shot of the day saw the ball whiz through the air and land in the fairway. He walked off the tee, strutted down the fairway and hit a wedge approach to eight feet. Fitzgerald took the Stars and Stripes cover off his player's putter. When he rolled in the birdie putt, McIlroy's lead over Yang had increased to nine strokes.

'Let them catch you, buddy,' came a cry from behind the ropes. McIlroy didn't flinch, didn't acknowledge the call. He had no intention of letting anybody get close to him.

On the fourth hole, McIlroy — as all great champions somehow managed to do at some stage or another — rode his luck. He hit his three-wood off the tee and then watched as his ball pitched into the primary rough but, rather than being buried, it kicked out into the secondary rough and then on to the fairway. He made the most of his good fortune when he hit his approach to 10 feet and sank the birdie putt. He had reached 16-under-par for the championship — another record.

When McIlroy looked towards the leaderboard, it told him that he had opened a 10-stroke lead on his pursuers.

McIlroy didn't get another birdie on the front nine, whilst Y.E. Yang showed his resilience with birdies on the sixth and ninth to remind the Ulsterman that he hadn't gone away. McIlroy's response to Yang's mini-fightback was to seal the deal in the most imperious way.

On the 214 yard par 3 10th hole, Yang exerted more pressure when he hit his tee shot to four feet. McIlroy, in response, took a six-iron from Fitzgerald and sent his shot from the elevated tee down towards the flag. It finished a mere six inches from the cup, and from there on home McIlroy's was a coronation march where the new king was given a standing ovation from tee to green and from green to tee.

The final stroke, when it came, was a tap-in on the 18th. It was the 268th stroke of McIlroy's march to glory and gave him an eight-shot winning margin over Australian Jason Day. Yang fell back into a four-way tie for third place after McIlroy's hammer-blow on the 10th hole was followed by a couple of bogeys on the back nine for the Korean.

As McIlroy left the 18th green for a final time, he embraced his father Gerry. 'Happy Father's Day,' he said.

McIlroy, at 22 years and 46 days, had become the youngest

European player on the modern European Tour to win a maiden Major. He broke the previous record of Seve Ballesteros who was 22 and 103 days when he won the British Open in 1979.

The manner of McIlroy's win was spellbinding, and also record-breaking. He had played golf of a quality never before seen in a us Open. Number 5600 River Road, the official address of Congressional Country Club in Bethesda, had never seen anything like it. But then neither had anywhere else. McIlroy announced his coming-of-age in record-breaking fashion and with a flair which none of the game's greats had ever managed.

Not Nicklaus.

Not Woods.

Not anyone!

———

Rory McIlroy had read the note from Graeme McDowell on his locker shortly before he went out to the driving range. 'It meant a lot to me,' recalled McIlroy, as he followed in G-Mac's shoes as the us Open champion.

Two successive champions from one small country; it was, as McDowell pointed out, akin to buying a lottery ticket. And winning!

On the Monday after his us Open win, McIlroy headed on to Massachusetts for a company day with Audemar Piquet, the luxury watch manufacturer. It was an indication of the huge financial benefits which professional golfers enjoy in their association with sponsors.

McIlroy was one to keep his feet firmly on the ground. As he attested: 'I am privileged to play golf for a living. The golf course is my office. But on the course I never think about money.'

In a year when the great Severiano Ballesteros passed away after a battle with brain cancer, the US Open win signalled the arrival of a new golfing superstar from Europe. But, as Chubby Chandler observed in the minutes following McIlroy's *tour de force* at Congressional, McIlroy was a player who transcended international borders.

His was a global appeal. 'I think he is going to be worldwide in popularity. Seve was Spanish, but he was everybody's. Rory is Irish, but everyone takes to him,' said Chandler.

McIlroy sought to get his head around his accomplishment as he kept the US Open trophy in close proximity. 'If you had asked me when I turned pro when I was 18, do you think you'd win a Major by the time you're 22, I would have said no. I would have liked to have been an established player on the European Tour, maybe (have) a couple of wins. But to contend in the Majors how I have so early, I don't really know what I can put it down to, if it's just hard work and practice or if I feel like I just have a little bit more focus or intensity for Major weeks. I'm not too sure.

'I'm surprised that I've done it so early. But it's great. It's a great thing for me. I can always call myself a Major champion now and I can go ahead and focus on, as I said, trying to get some more.

'All I wanted to do was play golf when I was growing up. I wanted to become the best that I could be. I probably said back then, I want to try to become the best in the world. In some ways I'm on my way to trying to do that.'

Gerry McIlroy has kept a photograph of his young son Rory. In it, the boy — all of 21 months old and wearing a sweater knitted by his mother Rosie — is swinging a golf club. Destiny had called him early.

A number of years later, Rory McIlroy appeared on the *Gerry Kelly Show* on Ulster Television. In his first appearance on TV, the boy — who had just won the World Under 10 Junior Championship at the Doral resort in Miami, Florida — chipped one ball after another into the drum of a washing machine.

McIlroy was a wunderkind who turned into a golfing phenomenon in his teenage years. To enable their son to pursue his dream, his father worked two jobs — as the caretaker in the local sports club and as a barman in Holywood Golf Club — and his mother worked night shifts in a factory. Their son was brought all over Ireland and to the United States to play in amateur championships.

The evidence of McIlroy's inexorable rise in golf is displayed much like a picture essay around the walls of his home club in Holywood: there are scorecards recording the various course records he achieved at Royal Portrush; a signed replica flag from the British Open at Carnoustie in 2007 when he was leading amateur medallist; a photograph from the 2007 Walker Cup, his last amateur engagement; and a framed photocopy of an old newspaper article relating his achievement in winning the world juniors as a nine-year old.

Memorabilia from the US Open triumph at Congressional simply confirmed his Major status.

Holywood was where it all started, when he towed along behind his father to the club and used plastic clubs with a plastic ball and spent his time chipping and putting on the green whilst his father and club professional Michael Bannon worked on the elder McIlroy's game. By seven he had his own cut-down clubs and real golf balls; by nine he was winning the world juniors; and by 15 he had become the youngest ever winner of the Irish Close Amateur Championship.

From those pre-teen years, McIlroy's swing was entrusted to Michael Bannon. And so it has stayed, the club professional the constant in the development of McIlroy's silky swing. From the time he first took up a club, sampling other sports but always returning to the Royal and Ancient game, McIlroy always wanted to play golf . . . and golf . . . and golf! It was what he was destined to do.

As a youngster, his first golfing hero was Nick Faldo. Then in 1997 Tiger Woods came along to win the Masters by 12 strokes and the young McIlroy was allowed to stay up late to watch on television. McIlroy was eight at the time, but to this day he can remember each and every shot which Woods played that day. He was inspired.

Throughout his amateur days McIlroy was a very special talent. In 2005, he became the youngest ever winner of the Irish Amateur Close Championship when it was held at Westport Golf Club. The following year, when it was staged at the European Club in Co. Wicklow, he became the first player since the legendary Joe Carr to retain it. Also in 2006, he won the European Amateur Stroke Play championship, and in 2007 claimed the Silver Medal as leading amateur in the British Open at Carnoustie where he was one of those by the 18th green when Pádraig Harrington ended the 60-year drought since an Irishman had last won a Major.

Having represented Britain and Ireland in the Walker Cup at Royal County Down in September of 2007, McIlroy made the long-anticipated move into the professional ranks. Although he had to rely on sponsors' invites to play on the European Tour, he won his full tour card in just his second appearance when he finished third in the Dunhill Links. It meant he didn't need to attend the Qualifying School — known as the 'torture chamber' to aspiring pros — and, in effect, ensured a seamless move from the amateur to the professional ranks.

McIlroy took his love of golf from his father, a low-figure handicapper who was also introduced to the sport in Holywood. But he has also proven to be his own man. Whilst his father has sported a Manchester City head cover on his driver, the son's soccer fixation is for rivals Manchester United.

He also demonstrated an awareness of change when the need arose as he sought to get the most from his talent: he took on J. P. Fitzgerald as caddie — replacing Gordon Faulkner — towards the end of the 2008 season; he started working with physical trainer Steve McGregor to improve his strength and conditioning; and he commenced work with putting guru Dave Stockton after the 2011 Masters tournament.

'If I look back on my career in 20 years, it's very possible that that day in Augusta probably was the defining moment, the point where I reached a crossroads. I could keep going the one way or really take responsibility for myself and say, right, this is what I need to do to get better and win and improve myself as a player. The Masters was huge for me. It was a huge disappointment at the time but, looking back on it, it probably was the most important day of my career so far.'

McIlroy first worked with Fitzgerald in the middle of 2008 when, as the player reminded anyone who would listen, he was ranked 200th in the world. 'He's helped bring me to where I am. He's been with me through some tough play-off losses. He's been with me through everything. It's the same with the situation with my coach. If it's not broke, don't fix it. J. P.'s one of my closest friends.'

The one constant on the coaching front throughout has been Michael Bannon, the PGA club professional who taught McIlroy from a very young age and developed the swing that brought him to that maiden Major in Congressional.

Chapter 8 ~

DESTINY'S CHILD ANSWERS THE CALL

140th Open Championship, Royal St George's
Golf Club, Sandwich, Kent, England

July 2011

O n the eve of the 140th Open championship, Darren Clarke had a special date. Well, a golfing date. The alarm clock sounded at the unearthly hour of 4.50 am and he was on the links at Royal St George's Golf Club — commonly known as Sandwich — bright and early for a pre-arranged practice round with Rory McIlroy.

Just like Tiger Woods had done for so many years, the early morning excursion was planned to get as much work done as possible in peace and relative quiet before the huge crowds descended on the links. Clarke was playing the role of facilitator. McIlroy, winner of the US Open just a month earlier, was the subject of global publicity exposure and there was a sense that the elder Ulsterman was doing his bit to put a protective arm around his young protégé.

On the 11th hole, the Northern Irish duo met up with Louis Oosthuizen and Charl Schwartzel. At the time, all four were part of the International Sports Management (ISM) stable of golfers and a friendly bet was struck. Of the quartet, Clarke — at 42 years of age — was comfortably the oldest, a grizzled veteran who had been a hero of so many European Ryder Cup teams, most notably at the K Club in Ireland in 2006, and also a multiple winner of World Golf Championships in an honour-laden career.

It wasn't his age which set Clarke apart from the others on that day. He was the only one of the four who hadn't won a Major championship. McIlroy had won the US Open in record-breaking fashion at Congressional a matter of weeks earlier; Schwartzel had birdied the last four holes of his final round to win the US Masters the previous April; and Oosthuizen had set the ball rolling by winning the previous year's British Open at St Andrews and had arrived at Sandwich as the defending champion.

Clarke's competitive spirit was such that even a bet struck on a few holes of a practice round focused the mind, and so it was as the two Northern Irishmen teamed up to take on the two South Africans. 'I was quick to suggest a game when I had Rory as my partner,' observed Clarke, with the smile of a man who had pocketed a few of Her Majesty's sterling pounds when the dry run was completed.

'We won enough,' responded Clarke, when asked how much he had taken from Schwartzel and Oosthuizen.

And yet the smile on Clarke's face that Wednesday morning didn't tell the whole story. He was irked in the way that the two younger Ulstermen in the field — McIlroy and Graeme McDowell, winners of the past two US Open championships — were subjected to scrutiny and roundly acknowledged as genuine contenders for the season's third Major. It was almost as if he were an afterthought.

The point was rubbed home to some extent with the advance publicity promoting a documentary on BBC Northern Ireland Television about the preparations and prospects of McIlroy and McDowell in the Open. When Clarke bumped into Stephen Watson, one of the most genial and exuberant men in the media and the voice of the documentary, the golfer chided the broadcaster as to why he too hadn't been included. It seemed good-natured banter, but there was an undercurrent. Clarke didn't like being the forgotten man, as if his time had passed.

Watson responded to the banter with a smile of his own, and a comment that he would make a documentary on Clarke — just as he'd done the previous year after McDowell's win at Pebble Beach and also the previous month after McIlroy's at Congressional —after he won that week's Open. Little could he have known!

Clarke's mood on that day wasn't helped either by the fact that the group of golf writers who surrounded him after he completed his practice round wanted to know more about McIlroy than they did about him.

When he was asked a question about how he had first met McIlroy, Clarke's response was frank and honest. 'Listen, I'm not going down that sycophantic route. Just calm yourself. He's playing fantastic and taking everything in his stride as you would expect,' said Clarke, serving as protector to McIlroy — who hadn't played a competitive round since his US Open win — but at the same time making it clear that he too was in the championship.

After all, Clarke had always gone into any tournament he entered with designs on winning. This was evident from his amateur days, when he won numerous championships around

Ireland, and of his haste to join the pro circuit. He had joined the paid ranks rather than wait for a call-up to the Walker Cup match at Portmarnock Golf Club in 1991 and his decision had been vindicated by the ease with which he made the transition and by the number of titles he collected around the world.

Then, when asked another McIlroy-related question, about how his ball flight was suited to windy conditions, Clarke again cut loose. 'Listen, I'm not going to stand here and gush about him any more. So, just calm down a little.'

It was different when the questions moved away from McIlroy.

Of his own game, Clarke — who had played a practice round with his good friend Lee Westwood on Tuesday and with McIlroy on Wednesday — didn't pull any punches. He said: 'To compete and to contend this week, not only are you going to have to play well, but you're going to have to putt very well because everyone is going to miss greens around this golf course . . . and especially with the breeze. You're going to have to up-and-down it very well and the greens are undulating, to say the least. So it will be tough. The golf course can make you look very silly if you get it wrong. I haven't quite got my feel. It just isn't there at the minute. At least it hasn't been for the last couple of days. But it could be (in time for the championship). My own game is okay. I'm not putting very well, but tee to green is very good. So we'll see. I might hole some this week.'

———

The names of those who had conquered Royal St George's was virtually a who's who of golf, even if Jack Nicklaus — the greatest Major winner of all — had never quite managed it. From

J. H. Taylor to Harry Vardon, Walter Hagen to Henry Cotton, Bobby Locke to Sandy Lyle, and Greg Norman to perhaps the unlikeliest of them all, Ben Curtis, the links in the south-eastern corner of England had managed to torment and tantalise and to produce worthy champions.

The links had another claim to fame. Thinly disguised as St Mark's in Ian Fleming's novel *Goldfinger*, it was the scene for one of the most famous fictional golf matches of all, between James Bond and Auric Goldfinger.

If that duel between 007 and Goldfinger — the golfing contest took up three chapters of the novel — offered fictionalised drama from the Sandwich links, the 13 occasions in which the course had played host to the British Open prior to 2011 provided real life drama that sometimes beggared belief, none more so than in 2003 when an unheralded Curtis — a 500-1 shot with the bookmakers and playing in his first ever Major — finished a stroke clear of Thomas Bjørn and Vijay Singh.

In his own way, Curtis exemplified the *raison d'être* for the championship itself. Ostensibly open to any golfer, professional or amateur, the American only qualified for the British Open by finishing in a share of 13th place at the Western Open two weeks before the Major. He didn't even own a passport at the time, but once he got his documentation sorted, Curtis made use of it and arrived at Sandwich before any other player, acquired a local caddie and — aside from one day's sightseeing in London — played more practice rounds on the course than any other player.

The caddie, Andy Sutton, schooled Curtis in the art of links golf, of bumping and running and of how to ignore the bad bounces that seaside golf invariably threw at a player. For three days Curtis stayed very much under the radar. On Saturday night, he told his fiancée Candace, who has since become his wife, that he thought he could win.

On Sunday, he leapfrogged player after player with an outward run of 32 strokes and, despite professing to shaking in his boots as he dropped shots close to home, Curtis — the only player in the field to finish under par — held his nerve to hole a six-foot par putt on the last to claim one of the unlikeliest Major wins ever. 'A good old country kid from the middle of nowhere', is how his father Bob would later describe Ben.

Nobody could ever describe his predecessor as the champion at Royal St George's as being a kid from nowhere. Greg Norman, so good that the moniker the 'Great White Shark' was created for him as his name became a multimillion business in itself, won in 1993 with a scintillating final round that enabled him to overhaul Nick Faldo.

Norman had started the final round one shot behind Faldo — who gained a measure of revenge some years later at the 1996 US Masters at Augusta National — and played like a man inspired, with the legendary Gene Sarazen describing the Aussie's swashbuckling closing 64 as 'awesome'.

'In my whole career, I'd never before gone round a golf course and not mishit a single shot. I was playing a game of chess, hitting the ball into position in the fairway where I could get it to the best spot on the green. I didn't want the round to end. I wished it could have been 36 holes,' said Norman, who'd actually missed a putt of no more than 14 inches on the 17th. Norman's rounds of 66-68-69-64 for a 72-hole total of 267 constituted a record low score for the championship.

Royal St George's had produced an international mix of champions prior to 2011: three Americans — Walter Hagen (1922 and 28), Bill Rogers (81) and Curtis (2003); four English champions — J. H. Taylor (1894), Harry Vardon (1899 and 1911), Henry Cotton (34) and Reg Whitcombe (38); two Scots — Jack White (1904) and Sandy Lyle (85); one South African — Bobby Locke (49) ; and one Australian — Norman (93).

Of all those wins, perhaps the most unusual was Vardon's in 1911, his second at Royal St George's and the third of his four British Open successes. That was the only time in the Major's history that a play-off did not go the full distance after Frenchman Arnaud Massy conceded the title to Vardon.

Scheduled for 36 holes, Massy found himself well behind as he played the 17th — the 35th — for the second time that day. Massy's total after 34 holes was 148 strokes and he was in trouble on what should have been the penultimate hole. When Vardon holed out on the 35th, his total was 143 and, realising the hopelessness of his situation, Massy picked up his ball and conceded the championship. The pair had finished the 72 holes on 303, one shot clear of Harold Hilton and Sandy Herd.

Apart from Vardon, the only other repeat champion over the course was the American Hagen. He won his first title on the links in 1922, becoming the first US-born player to win the British Open. Hagen started the final round two shots adrift of Scots-born American Jock Hutchison, who was defending the title he'd won at St Andrews the previous year. But Hutchison finished with a closing 76 and Hagen's 72 — the lowest of the championship — allowed him to claim a one-stroke winning margin over England's Jim Barnes.

Six years later, Hagen — travelling across the Atlantic in a luxury liner — returned to Royal St George's and again conquered the links. His preparations for the 1928 British Open hadn't gone too well: he lost an exhibition match to Archie Compston by 18 and 17 (over a four-round encounter). Hagen turned around his game for the real thing, returning rounds of 75-73-72-72 for a total of 292 to claim his third of four British Opens with a two-stroke winning margin over Gene Sarazen.

Probably the hardest-won title of all over the Sandwich links was that of Reg Whitcombe in 1938, when a fierce storm wreaked havoc in the final round. The exhibition tent and much of the merchandise on display were destroyed, with debris flying across the course as far as Prince's, almost a mile way. Of the 37 players who made the cut, 24 of them failed to break 80 in either of their final two rounds. Whitcombe closed with rounds of 75 and 78 for a total of 295, two shots clear of Jimmy Adams.

Quirky was one word used to describe the Royal St George's links. There were others. Bumpy. Humpy. Unfair. For, of all the courses on the British Open rotation, the landscape that in comments was often referred to as resembling that of a moonscape was one that continually frustrated players. In fact, the R&A stayed away for over 30 years — keeping it off the championship rota from 1949 to 1981 — as they tired of player complaints about several holes with blind shots and, on its staging in 2003, Fred Funk — normally a polite and courteous soul, remarked, 'I shouldn't say I hated the golf course, but I hated the golf course . . . It is nearly impossible to keep a ball in play.'

For the 140th edition of golf's oldest Major championship — which came on the back of a lengthy dry spell — the fairways were firm, but there was none of the rough which caused such heavy penalties to wayward drives some eight years earlier. One of the early victims on that occasion had been world No. 1 Tiger Woods, who lost a ball on the very first hole and ran up a triple-bogey seven.

Players who headed into the 2011 Open were faced with a firm course. Although 2.6 inches of rain had fallen in June, it came too late to beef up the rough. There was only 1.3 inches of rain from March to May (against the norm of 5.8 inches) and the result was a firm course that brought its infamous bumps more into play than ever.

Curtis, the man who conquered the links in 2003, talked of the challenges that players faced. 'You've got to stay out of those bunkers! But the biggest thing is controlling the flight of your ball, especially if the wind gets up. If you can't keep the ball down or control your flight or hit the shots you want, then you're in trouble,' remarked Curtis.

The same challenge it had always presented, in other words.

The links was discovered by a Scottish surgeon, Laidlaw Purves, who had actually visited England's south coast with his brother, Alexander, to see where the Roman emperor Claudius had landed in A.D. 43. The history lesson became secondary when Purves, a keen golfer, found himself on a stretch of untouched linksland. And, in 1887, Purves, along with his friend Henry Lamb, a wine merchant, and another London-based Scot, William Anderson, founded St George's Golf Club on land leased from the Earl of Guilford with a farmhouse as a ready-made clubhouse.

Ramsay Hunter, a greenkeeper, was brought down from Scotland to help sculpt the course, and Purves, who had no experience of golf course architecture, took it upon himself to do the layout. He was aided by natural terrain that lent itself to the construction of holes, and within five years of opening it was rewarded with the British Amateur championship. In 1894 it was given the Open championship itself and J. H. Taylor became the first winner over the course.

The length of the course had naturally increased over time. King Edward VII granted it royal status in 1902, a time when the rubber-core ball revolutionised the game, and a handful of holes were altered as it grew to a length of 6,594 yards when it played host to the 1911 championship. By the time of the 140th Open championship, its yardage had increased to 7,211. But the routing and layout remained the same as that first created by Purves well over a century previously.

————

Darren Clarke's irritability at being constantly questioned about Rory McIlroy was understandable. And McIlroy's official press conference demonstrated how his appeal had moved beyond Ulster, Ireland, the United Kingdom and Europe. His US Open win had catapulted him into the role of golf's newest global superstar and the tented conference room was packed to capacity with a live feed to American TV channel ESPN, which only served to reaffirm his new status.

That Tiger Woods had pulled out of the championship due to injury only increased the spotlight on McIlroy. Woods had sprained a ligament in his knee joint playing from an awkward lie at the Masters in April and aggravated the injury at the Players in May. Woods — who had missed the US Open — announced his decision not to play in a statement on his website. 'I am only going to come back when I'm 100 per cent ready. I do not want to risk further injury.'

McIlroy's explosion on to the international stage meant Woods's absence was not the news it once would have been. A new kid had arrived on the block. Since he had won his US Open title, the Ulsterman had stayed away from tournament play but seemed to have enjoyed life to the full: he attended a heavyweight boxing bout in Germany and appeared in the royal box at Wimbledon.

When he arrived at Royal St George's, McIlroy became the centre of attention rather than being a sports fan. He made a very late arrival to Sandwich, which surprised many other professionals, but he had practised over the links in relative peace and quiet the previous week.

'I didn't realise how much of a fuss it would create, or how much of a buzz,' said McIlroy of his US Open win, adding: 'The support I've had from people at home, from everyone all over the world, has been pretty overwhelming. (But) it's a nice feeling to have that support walking on to the golf course.'

In actual fact, McIlroy's late arrival in Kent followed a formula similar to the one he adopted at St Andrews in 2010 (where he led after the first round and eventually finished in third). The player opted not to play in the previous week's Scottish Open and instead paid a two-day visit to prepare away from the madding crowds. He then fine-tuned his game on the Monday night with a nine-hole run around Royal County Down with his father Gerry, when he carried his own clubs.

'I've got back into my own routine, been practising a lot,' said McIlroy who had been the story at each of the year's two previous Majors: in the Masters, he had suffered a final round meltdown, and in the US Open he had decimated the field. 'I feel as if my preparation has been really good coming in. It was nice to relax and take it all in after the US Open, but I knew that the time for reflection wasn't really at this point of the season. It's at the end. I've got to forget what happened three weeks ago (at Congressional) and just come in and try to win another golf tournament.'

Of past close calls in the Majors and his elevation to that of champion, McIlroy remarked: 'I learned a lot from the Open at St Andrews (in 2010), shooting that great first round and then not handling the weather too well on the second day. And I had a really good chance of winning going into the last round of the PGA (at Whistling Straits). I was tied for the lead with four holes to go. And then the Masters, leading going into the last.

'It's been a gradual process and I've learnt every time, and it's maybe taken me three or four times to put all the pieces together. Now I feel like I've basically learnt most of the lessons that I needed to learn to get me over the line, especially in a Major championship, and I feel as if I'll be able to go on and contend a lot more.'

Certainly, his was the name on everyone's lips as the 140th Open Championship got under way. Barely anyone mentioned Darren Clarke as a possible winner.

————

Graeme McDowell arrived in Sandwich sporting a healthy growth of facial hair, fast moving from designer stubble into a fully fledged beard. His physical appearance was one thing, but it was the mental release of arriving into the Open as someone not burdened by the expectation of others as a reigning Major champion that seemed to bring a freshness back to his demeanour.

G-Mac's breakthrough Major win in the US Open at Pebble Beach had meant he arrived into the British Open at St Andrews, the US PGA at Whistling Straits and the US Masters at Augusta National, saddled with a status that heaped pressure on him. His bid for another Major started in earnest at Royal St George's.

As usual, McDowell was articulate and honest in his assessment of his game as he prepared to take on the quirky challenges of the bone-hard links in Sandwich. 'Everything I touched in 2010 turned to gold, but my game this year has not gone quite as well. But I feel in good shape. The game's giving me a few kicks at the minute. I'm quietly very happy and I'm trying to stay patient and I know you have to take the rough with the smooth. Last year was smooth. This year's been up and down, but I'm grafting away and working hard.'

It hadn't been a bad year for McDowell, just that it was hard to repeat the many highs of 2010 when he'd not only won the US Open but also played the superhero role for Europe in the Ryder Cup when he won the vital singles match with American Hunter Mahan.

Although his 2011 season had not matched his efforts of the previous year, there had been weeks when he had contended: in the Players championship at Sawgrass, McDowell had gone into the final round as leader, only to implode with a closing 79 that saw him fall from first down to 33rd; and he had also challenged in his defence of the Wales Open and in the Scottish Open, only for one poor round on each occasion to be his undoing.

McDowell had high hopes that the Open would mark a return to his real self. 'I certainly haven't felt this good in a while coming into a Major, since Pebble (Beach) probably.'

He wasn't the only one who teed off with fresh hope. Louis Oosthuizen, winner of the Claret Jug in St Andrews the year before, had struggled to reclaim the form in the Majors that had seen him make that breakthrough win over the Old Course.

'I'm just trying to get into that same rhythm I had going into the Open last year,' said Oosthuizen, who added: 'Every Major you tee off, you just want to try and find the game. I didn't go in with great form into the Open last year but found a few things on Monday and Tuesday while practising and just played really nicely the whole week, found my rhythm very well and the swing. And just putted beautifully.'

Oosthuizen had travelled in to Kent on a special charter flight from the John Deere Classic on the US Tour and professed to having mixed feelings as his reign came to an end. 'It's sad and it's a relief in the same sentence. It's always nice, the feeling of (being) an Open champion. It's a great honour. But from here on out, you're not the Open champion any more. Well, unless . . .'

Briefly, he allowed himself to think of Pádraig Harrington, who had managed to retain the Claret Jug at Royal Birkdale in 2008 a year after he won for the first time in Carnoustie.

———

Those who teed up in the first round of the 140th Open were given stark reminders that a golfing legend had passed on from this world. Iconic images of Seve Ballesteros, who had died in May after a long battle with brain cancer, were mounted on hoardings around the course and most prominently around the grandstand by the 18th green.

The huge crowds who flocked to Sandwich on Thursday didn't get what they expected. If they'd made the journey in their droves to hail golf's newest superhero — a certain Mr McIlroy — the first round contrived to give them a blast from the past in the shape of Thomas Bjørn, and a sense of the future in English amateur Tom Lewis.

Bjørn had made a calamitous finish to the 2003 Open and only got a late ticket into the field after Vijay Singh withdrew injured. It was too early to believe that Bjørn — whose father had died in June — was due a form of payback for the way the course had treated him all of eight years previously, but his opening round 65, five-under-par, provided some redemption.

The Great Dane wasn't alone at the top, though. Late in the day, a sting in the tail was provided by Tom Lewis, a 20-year-old English amateur half the age of Bjørn, who benefited from a late start by which time the winds that had buffeted the morning starters had all but disappeared. He too shot a 65, and the co-leaders had one shot to spare over Americans Lucas Glover and Webb Simpson and Spain's Miguel Ángel Jiménez.

The quartet of Irish players in the field fared well, in the main. Darren Clarke, who had rediscovered the unique characteristics of links golf since he'd moved home to Portrush in 2010, and Graeme McDowell — who again showed his fortitude by recovering from a potentially damaging double-bogey at his very first hole — each shot 68s, while Rory McIlroy, playing in the more difficult morning conditions, opened with a 71.

Pádraig Harrington would have preferred to talk post-round about his birdies, rather than his flat cap — which he wore to raise awareness about testicular cancer — which had become something of an internet sensation during his opening round. Unfortunately for the Dubliner, birdies were a scarce commodity in a round of 73.

The weather and the course combined to create numerous twists and turns. And, as heart-warming as Bjørn's renaissance and the unlikely contention of Lewis, who earned his ticket through the minefield of qualifying, there was also a sense of well-being about Clarke's revival. Just as one swallow didn't make a summer, one good round didn't cure all of a player's problems. But there was something about Clarke's demeanour that hinted that all was well with the world.

Clarke, who had only started working again with the famed sports psychologist Dr Bob Rotella on his arrival in Sandwich, always loved seaside golf. Although he first played out of Dungannon Golf Club when he took up the sport, much of his teenage years were spent on the famed links of Royal Portrush Golf Club on the Causeway Coast, and his return to live there had shown him what he had been missing.

'Anytime I step back on links, I always enjoy it. This one is particularly difficult because of the undulation in the fairways and the demand that puts on the second shots. It's just a real, real tough and stern test. You've got to stay patient, which has not always been one of my strong points,' said Clarke.

Clarke mixed five birdies with three bogeys in his 68 and appeared invigorated 'The Open is the biggest and best tournament in the world. It's the only Major that's played on the turf that the game was started on . . . Why wouldn't I enjoy it?' he said.

Nobody played as well on the homeward journey as McDowell, who covered the back nine in a mere 31 strokes. 'The putter kept me in there. So back in 31 was a pretty nice effort. It should make dinner taste pretty good. Thankfully I managed to get things back on track,' he conceded.

The putter that had served McDowell so well had received something of a facelift in the run-up to the championship. And to good effect, as the Ulsterman overcame a potentially disastrous opening double-bogey to return a 68. 'It's the same putter with a little bit more weight on the sole and I changed the grip after about two years. There was a lot of blood, sweat and tears on the grip. I didn't want to change it, but I haven't been putting well lately and I wanted to inject a little bit of magic back into the putter,' said McDowell.

That Thursday, though, belonged in the main to Bjørn and Lewis. They couldn't have been more different: Bjørn was chairman of the Players Committee on the PGA European Tour, while Lewis had left school at the age of 16 to play golf full-time and had his heart set on playing for Great Britain and Ireland in the Walker Cup match against the United States.

Of his decision to swap schoolbooks for the golf course, Lewis remarked: 'I was dyslexic and didn't really enjoy that side of it. I'm just trying to live as normal a life as possible, but golf is my career and that's what I needed to do and work hard at it. So, hopefully

I can carry on doing what I'm doing because it obviously seems to be working right.'

In shooting the lowest ever round by an amateur in the Open, Lewis also became the first amateur since Michael Bonallack in 1968 to share the first round lead.

The contrast between Lewis and Bjørn couldn't have been starker.

Bjørn, at 40, had history with Royal St George's. In 2003, he seemed destined to win the Claret Jug when he led by three shots with four holes to go. But the run for home proved to be a catalogue of errors. It was to be the closest Denmark's greatest player ever got to winning a Major, although he did subsequently finish runner-up to Phil Mickelson in the 2005 US PGA.

That was the year — 2005 — when Bjørn, 12 months after walking off the course at the K Club citing 'demons' in his head, also contrived to run up a septuple-bogey 11 at the 17th in the final round of the European Open when it seemed he had the title within his grasp. So golf had often used Bjørn as its fall guy.

That first round at Sandwich was like a blast from the past for Bjørn. 'I've always promised myself I will keep going and keep going. You try to make the best of every single day and that's what I have done. I don't play the golf that I used to, but I did today. But most of the time I don't. That's down to a lot of issues, I think. Losing the golf swing over a couple of seasons where I found golf extremely difficult, where when you were younger you probably found it a little easier. There's a lot of issues. But I always look ahead. I'm 40 years old, and there might just be a little bit more in me,' said Bjørn.

Indeed, Bjørn's endeavours hadn't gone unnoticed. As Rory McIlroy and Ernie Els stood on the 11th tee, the two looked at the leaderboard to see Bjørn's name at the top. 'What is he doing? How is he six-under-par?' they asked each other, all the time shaking their heads.

———

Humour can be the best medicine of all. On the Friday of the second round, Darren Clarke took his place on the first tee and started to do a stretching routine that enabled ageing muscles and limbs to keep pace with the new finely honed athlete that was making professional golf a chosen sport.

As Clarke stretched and bent over, someone in the grandstand behind the tee box gave a loud, shrill wolf whistle that prompted the gallery to break into laughter.

'I hope that's a lady,' quipped Clarke.

The response was another wolf whistle from a man in the stands. Clarke joined in the laughter.

The precursor to his round brought some light relief, but Clarke's endeavours in the second round brought genuine applause from one and all in the grandstands by the 18th green where Ballesteros's image served as a reminder of past great deeds.

Clarke sank a birdie putt on the 18th green that allowed him to sign for a second successive round of 68 for a midway total of 136, four-under-par. The round had been far from straightforward and featured a double-bogey and an eagle in the space of four holes on his front nine.

Where had this resurgence come from? It was hard to explain, given his results in the run-up. Although he had won the Iberdola

Open in Mallorca, Spain, earlier in the season, Clarke's form going into the Open was far from impressive: tied-45th at the BMW PGA at Wentworth; 63rd at the Wales Open; a missed cut at the French Open; and tied-66th at the previous week's Scottish Open.

For some reason, Clarke's attitude at Sandwich was as relaxed as he had ever been on a golf course. Perhaps it had to do with teaming up with Rotella again, even if the sports psychologist was a house guest of Pádraig Harrington for the week.

Clarke's press conference after his second round provided an insight into his mindset.

Why was there such a big gap in meeting up with Rotella?

Clarke: Probably 4,000 miles.

Could you not use video link technology?

Clarke: No, not really.

Did anyone take his place?

Clarke: Many have tried . . . I've broken many of them, thank you. But Dr Bob? His thought process is very simple, and that seems to suit me.

And, later, when it was put to him that his manager Chubby Chandler had talked of putting Clarke on a diet, he replied: 'Chubby has always said that I play better fat, so I've obviously been adhering to that theory. He has been going on at me about points and Weight Watchers and everything. And after seeing myself on television, he might have a point!'

On a more serious note, Clarke had let his clubs do the talking for the first two days and had put himself in a position to challenge for the championship he always ranked as 'the greatest' of all. Throughout his career, Clarke had won two WGCS — including staring down Tiger Woods in his prime — and claimed tournaments all over the world. But a Major had proven elusive. His closest calls came in the Open at Troon in 1997 (when he was second) and the Open at Royal Lytham and St Annes in 2001 (when he was third).

Since 2007, he had seen Pádraig Harrington capture three Majors and, in little over a year, had also seen two of the players he himself inspired — Graeme McDowell and Rory McIlroy — claim Majors. 'I've been personally delighted for both of them. You know, we've got back-to-back US Open champions from a little, small country like Northern Ireland. That's a massive achievement. You can't explain how big that actually is. We've got two wonderful ambassadors for Northern Ireland in G-Mac and Rory and it's been great. So it hasn't really affected me apart from being proud that I'm from the same place as they are, and I may have given them a little bit of a helping hand here and there on the way up.'

Clarke, however, believed he had benefited from moving back home to Portrush in 2010 after living in London for the previous 13 years. 'It's a lot easier to play better whenever family life and stuff at home is much better, much more stable again,' said Clarke, whose first wife Heather died shortly before the Ryder Cup at the K Club in 2006. He was in a new relationship and had got engaged the previous Christmas to Alison Campbell, who ran her own model agency in Belfast. They married in April 2012.

As for the golf, Clarke always believed he would contend again in a Major. As he put it, 'If you ask any professional, whenever they're not playing as well as they think they should, we all get annoyed and frustrated. But I've been around the mill for a while. So I never really disappeared. I'm just trying to get it back out again. So far this week, I've played quite nicely.'

Clarke shared the midway lead with Glover, the US Open champion of 2009. But it was a congested leaderboard. The Irishman and the American were a shot clear of a quartet of players that included Bjørn, Chad Campbell, Martin Kaymer and Miguel Ángel Jiménez. Behind them, a sextet of players that included Masters champion Schwartzel were only another stroke behind. In all, only seven strokes separated all the players who survived into the final two rounds.

Inevitably, there were some significant casualties when the cut mark fell on 143, three-over. Both the world Nos 1 and 2 of the time — Luke Donald and Lee Westwood respectively — fell by the wayside before their challenge ever got going, while Harrington, McDowell, Els, Ian Poulter and Geoff Ogilvy were also sent packing.

There was, too, some old magic from none other than 61-year-old Tom Watson, who had the 15th hole-in-one of his career *en route* to making the cut. And, as if to prove that ageism didn't exist, 20-year-old amateur Tom Lewis also made the cut.

Clarke's move to the top of the leaderboard — a position he last held at Troon in 1997 — came after a 68 which included a remarkable eagle putt from over 100 feet on the seventh. Three holes earlier, Clarke had run up a double-bogey six on the fourth.

Only seven strokes covered the field going into the weekend, and McIlroy's assessment that it was a 'very open' Open served as a reminder that it was anyone's title.

But McDowell had faith in Clarke. 'Darren is a fantastic ball striker. He's a great links player, and he's the type of player that can still win golf tournaments,' said G-Mac.

Professional golfers young and old held a similar theory when it came to tee times. Basically, the view was that over any given season such start times tended to even themselves out. In Darren Clarke's case, it was his play over the first two days at Sandwich which ensured that he had a late afternoon start in the third round and, although he got under way in heavy rain, those earlier starters had endured much worse weather conditions.

Clarke was never one to moan or groan about playing in the wind or the rain, and on that day he simply got on with the job. After all, he was chasing the greatest prize of them all in his eyes. The Claret Jug, a trophy he'd pursued like the golden fleece for two full decades, had finally moved within tantalising reach.

The ugly squalls that hit the Kent coastline for much of the third round left players exasperated, and many felt as if they'd been in a heavyweight boxing match, so beat up were they by the time they reached the sanctuary of the locker room. Scores sky-rocketed into the 80s but, for Clarke, there was no such calamity: he signed for a 69 to go with the 68s of the previous two days and assumed sole occupation of the lead with a total of 205, five-under-par.

'If somebody had given me 69 before I was going out to play, I would have bitten their hand off for it. Saying that, we did get very fortunate with the draw. Sometimes, to win any tournament the draw can make a big difference. But in the Open championship it makes a huge difference. We got very lucky,' accepted Clarke, who was paired with Lucas Glover in the final group.

There were those who would have argued that he had made his own luck. Clarke was the only player all day to birdie the tough starting hole and, despite the rain, he and Glover talked throughout the round as if it provided relief from the weather conditions which severely tested the waterproofs and made the caddies' jobs even more difficult than normal.

Clarke had a fellow-Irishman on his bag. John Mulrooney, from Bray in Co. Wicklow, was an experienced bagman who numbered José María Olazábal, Miguel Ángel Jiménez and David Howell among his list of employers. He had teamed up with Clarke at the Iberdola Open in Mallorca just two months before Sandwich, and after Clarke won, the temporary arrangement was made more permanent.

Two weeks before the Open, Clarke and Mulrooney had travelled to Royal St George's for a practice round. 'It went well,' recalled Mulrooney of that reconnaissance visit.

On their arrival at the venue for the actual championship, though, the caddie got a feeling that something special was afoot when Clarke was given the same locker used by Greg Norman in the Australian's win in 1993. 'Even Tom Watson said it could be a lucky locker,' said Mulrooney.

Clarke relied on his exceptional ball-striking rather than mere luck as he worked his way around the course in the third round. After he sank a 12 footer for birdie on the first to prompt a huge roar from the galleries, the Ulsterman got the head down. He drove the ball well, but the key was superb iron play as he avoided any disasters and ran up just two bogeys to mix with three birdies in an impressive display.

'I couldn't have hit the ball any better from tee to green. That was about as good as I could do,' acknowledged Clarke, even if there were times once he reached the putting surface that he was guilty of some misreads. Nothing, though, got him down and he kept a smile on his face throughout all the wind and rain and whatever the weather gods threw at him.

Only three players managed to break par in the third round. The best round of the day came from the young American Rickie Fowler, who contrived to produce a 68 in the worst of the conditions. Fowler, who turned professional after the 2009 Walker Cup match, had been the top-ranked amateur in the world for much of 2007 and 08. He had moved seamlessly into the professional ranks.

Fowler and fellow-American Dustin Johnson each shot 68s on that miserable day to move on to the shoulders of Clarke. Fowler was two adrift alongside Thomas Bjørn, but Johnson — one of the longest hitters on tour — occupied second place on his own. He was one shot behind Clarke and had ghosts of his own to bury in the Majors.

In the 2010 US Open at Pebble Beach, Johnson had led by three strokes as he headed into the final round, but endured a horrendous start — which included a lost ball — and eventually signed for an 82 that left him some distance behind eventual champion Graeme McDowell. And, in the 2010 US PGA at Whistling Straits, Johnson held a one-stroke lead as he played the 18th hole in the final round. Unfortunately for him, he was penalised two strokes for grounding his club in an ill-defined 'bunker' and missed out by one shot on a play-off that saw Martin Kaymer defeat Bubba Watson.

Johnson preferred to take the approach that such set-backs had toughened him up for the challenge he faced at Sandwich, as he headed into the final round a shot behind Clarke. 'It doesn't matter whether you're chasing or have got the lead. I would rather have the lead, because it is one shot less I have to make up. But going out (in the final round) I am still going to have to play aggressively when I can and play smart when I have to. I've been in this situation a few times.'

Ironically, Clarke too had been in positions to win Majors in the past. Had he too learned lessons? 'The Open is the biggest and best tournament in the world. You know, I've failed 20 times. Well, 19 times I've failed to try and lift the Claret Jug . . . I'm very pleased to be leading going into the final round.'

It seemed that the deafening roars from the 18th green on that Saturday were still ringing in Clarke's ears as he assessed the position he had claimed with one round to go. 'Did I ever doubt I would get myself back into this position? No. Did I know it was going to happen? No. Did I hope it was going to happen? Yes. But did I ever doubt it? No.'

———

On the Sunday morning of the final round, Darren Clarke met with Dr Bob Rotella.

'You've got to feel like you are destined to win some of these,' the sports psychologist told the player.

'I know Doc,' replied Clarke. 'I want to go out there and trust myself and be happy for the whole 18 holes, and whatever happens happens — if I win or I don't win.'

Rotella reminded him of the importance of 'staying in the moment'. Easier said than done, of course, especially with the majority in the huge galleries who flocked to Royal St George's that day with Clarke — a pint-drinking, cigar-smoking man of the people — in pole position to deliver a long-anticipated victory.

And just as Clarke went about meeting up with Dustin Johnson for the final round, Rotella reminded him of one other thing: acceptance! As Rotella put it, 'Darren's tendency is to get down and beat himself up.' He didn't want that to happen in the final round of the British Open of all places.

Clarke had enjoyed a nice dinner in the ISM house on Saturday night, where Rory McIlroy was one of those to share the meal. There were good vibes, and why not? The ISM stable was on a roll since Louis Oosthuizen's win in the British Open at St Andrews the previous year. Charl Schwartzel had captured the Masters and McIlroy had won the US Open.

'I think they feed off each other. They eat together, they travel together, and they play practice rounds together,' observed ISM chief Chubby Chandler. Clarke had played practice rounds with Lee Westwood on Tuesday and with Rory McIlroy on Wednesday. 'I think that was a sign, playing with them, that he realised his game was up to it.'

The wise words of Rotella and Chandler were not the only ones which Clarke carried with him to the first tee. Tiger Woods, an old adversary going back to the time when Clarke had out-duelled him in the heat of battle at the WGC match play in 2000, had been unable to play in the championship due to injury. But Woods did send a text message to Clarke, one that urged him to finish the job he had started on Thursday.

Clarke had to stay strong in the final round, as gusts of wind coming in off the English Channel accentuated the challenge. His task was compounded too by a final round charge from Phil

Mickelson, who had dispatched his family to Paris for some cultural experiences as he concluded his preparations, which saw the left-hander nab four birdies and an eagle in the first 10 holes to jump into contention. He briefly shared the lead with Clarke, but he suffered four bogeys on the run for home and eventually finished in tied-second with Johnson.

After he holed a 12 footer for par on the first, Clarke settled to his task. He birdied the second (sand wedge to four feet) and bogeyed the fourth. On the 564 yard par 5 seventh hole, Clarke provided his answer to those who wanted to usurp him: there, he hit a perfect drive, and with 198 yards left to the pin, hit an eight-iron approach that landed 16 feet from the hole. He rolled in the eagle putt with authority.

It gave Clarke the lead again on his own, and he never relinquished it. Mickelson's charge — when he covered the front nine in a mere 30 strokes — petered out on the homeward run as he missed some short putts, and the American eventually signed for a 68, for 278.

Clarke kept a much closer eye on his other principal opponent, Johnson, who played alongside him. But Johnson's threat effectively disappeared on the 547 yard par 5 14th, where the long-hitting American — who had seen Clarke lay up with his own approach shot — went for the green in two. Johnson pushed his iron shot and the last he saw of it was as it sailed over the out-of-bounds white stakes.

There and then, Clarke knew all he had to do was get home safely. And he did, even if he finished bogey-bogey. The main thing was that he had kept any calamity off his card and his 70th stroke of the round and his 275th of the championship was no more than a tap-in from a matter of three inches as the huge roars around the 18th green confirmed he had achieved his destiny. When the numbers were totted up, Clarke had three strokes to spare over Johnson and Mickelson.

'It's been a dream since I was a kid to win the Open, like any kid's dream is,' said Clarke, who at 42 became the oldest British Open champion since Roberto de Vicenzo won at the age of 44 in 1967. And as he exited the 18th green to a huge ovation, he was involved in a number of bear hug embraces: one by one, his caddie John Mulrooney, his parents Godfrey and Hettie, his manager Chubby Chandler, his fiancée Alison. All took their turns.

His two teenage sons Tyrone and Conor had stayed at home in Portrush to watch their dad on television.

Phil Mickelson and his wife Amy — back from Paris — also made sure they were by the greenside to offer their congratulations. 'I'm really happy for him. He was one of the first people that called us, Amy and me, a couple of years ago (after Mickelson's wife was diagnosed with breast cancer). He's been through this and we couldn't have had a better person to talk to. It was fun to make a run at him . . . but I couldn't be happier for him,' said Mickelson.

Clarke appreciated the Mickelsons' gesture. 'Phil has been through an awful lot with Amy and what have you, and we have spoken quite a lot. He has also turned into a very good friend of mine through thick and thin. In the 2006 Ryder Cup at the K Club, the way that we walked out — the Europeans were alphabetical and the Americans were whatever way they qualified, so I was C, so I was on my own, and Amy and Phil were walking opposite me . . . and Amy stood in the middle and held both our hands. I can't say anything more about it than that.'

When the time came for Clarke to get his hands on the Claret Jug at the presentation ceremony, he could hardly contain his emotions. After years of toil and his share of personal heartbreak, Clarke — at the 20th time of asking — had arrived at golf's top table as a Major champion.

To do so, he'd shown self-belief and perseverance, having overcome personal trauma, and he used a wonderful talent that first surfaced as an 11-year old when his father Godfrey, a former soccer player with Dungannon Swifts in the Irish League, and mother Hettie took out family membership at Dungannon Golf Club.

'In terms of what's going through my heart, there's obviously somebody who is watching down from up above there. And I know she'd be very proud of me. She'd probably be saying, I told you so,' said an emotional Clarke in tribute to his late wife in his champion's speech.

Of his breakthrough Major win and how he managed to keep his emotions in check in getting the job finished, he explained: 'I'm just older, just a little bit older and allegedly a little bit wiser. But I certainly had a few thoughts going through my head when I was walking on to the green on 18 because, at that stage, I could have four putts from there. Even I figured I could manage to get down in four from the edge of the green there. But the few thoughts, thinking about the past, and then making a speech, I can only be as normal as I am. So if I didn't feel a little bit emotional it wouldn't quite be right.'

———

Darren Clarke had a choice to make in his teenage years: rugby or golf? The decision to play golf — a sport he'd taken up as an 11-year old when he progressed from caddying for his father to playing, was vindicated from an early stage as he set about dominating the amateur championships run by the Golfing Union of Ireland.

As an amateur, he excelled. Clarke won the Irish Close championship in 1990 — when he beat Pádraig Harrington in the final — and he also claimed the North, South and East of Ireland championship titles as well. But the amateur scene grew too small and a bigger world beckoned. He was certain to be picked for the Great Britain and Ireland team for the Walker Cup at Portmarnock in 1991, but decided to make the move into the professional ranks and joined the then fledgling International Sports Management agency established by former European Tour player Chubby Chandler.

Clarke's first win as a professional didn't come until he was three years into life on tour, at the 1993 Alfred Dunhill Open. It was to be a precursor to an honour-laden career that saw him win at least once every season from 1998 to 2003. Among those title wins was a victory over Tiger Woods in the 2000 Accenture World Match Play final and in the 2003 WGC-Bridgestone Invitational.

On tour he set targets. He became the first player on the European Tour to shoot 60 for a second time at the Smurfit European Open at the K Club in 1999. He had first accomplished the feat at the 1992 Monte Carlo Open. Ironically, he failed to win either event.

Personal tragedy, however, hit with the death of his wife Heather in 2006, just weeks before the Ryder Cup at the K Club.

Fittingly, Clarke — who played as one of captain Ian Woosnam's 'wild card' picks — managed to play a hugely significant role in Europe's win over the United States and emerged with an unbeaten record. He won all three of his matches.

After the death of his wife, Clarke — who set up the Darren Clarke Foundation to help develop junior golf in Ireland, and which also promoted breast cancer awareness — juggled the responsibility of raising his two sons Tyrone and Conor with life on tour. In 2008, he still managed to win twice: in the Dutch Open and the Asian Open.

In 2010, just as Pádraig Harrington had used the event as a stepping stone to Major wins, Clarke won the J. P McManus Invitational tournament in Adare Manor, Co. Limerick, which gave him a huge confidence boost. He finished runner-up in the following week's Scottish Open, which earned him a place in the following week's British Open. And a top-15 finish on the European Tour in 2011 gave him his ticket to the scene of his greatest triumph here at Royal St George's.

Clarke has a work hard, play hard attitude. 'I've always been generous rewarding myself with things. I've always liked the cars, wine and cigars. Now more than ever. We're only here once. You've just got to enjoy it. I don't look at myself as being famous. I'm just a golfer. I just like to go to the pub and have a pint of Guinness. That's me.'

Always known as a hard worker, his long-time sports psychologist Dr Karl Morris — with whom he wrote a best-selling book — once remarked: 'Darren's a massive perfectionist and that's what makes him work so hard. One of the bigger myths about Darren is that he doesn't work hard enough. But his idea of a day off is to play 36 holes. Darren knows how good he is and, without question, he is the most gifted player I have ever seen.'

Nobody impacted on Clarke more than his manager. 'He's worked really hard (to win a Major),' said Chandler. 'It's been a long road and we've had some dark phone calls. There was a time where you'd take a phone call and you just knew it wasn't a very good call . . . he lost about five or six years of his career. The psychologist Mike Finnegan gave him something which basically said, prove everybody wrong, and he's been doing that.'

At the bottom of it all, Clarke described himself as 'a bit of a normal bloke, aren't I, really? I like to go to the pub and have a pint, jump on Easy Jet, fly home, buy everybody a drink — just normal. There's not many airs and graces about me. I was just a little bit more difficult to deal with in my earlier years (on tour) and I've mellowed. I'm just a normal guy playing golf, having a bit of fun.'

Once Clarke was asked what characteristic he most disliked in others. 'The inability to see the bigger picture,' he replied, adding: 'Sometimes people need to step back and see what's really going on. I had to do that with my golf. But rudeness is my number one hate. Please and thank you are two of the easiest things in the world to say. I try to instil that in my two boys.'

Chapter 9 ~

BOY WONDER ROARS
ON THE SHORE

94th US PGA Championship, Kiawah Island,
South Carolina, USA

August 2012

The few people wandering the grounds of the Grove Hotel, a luxury establishment in Hertfordshire, outside London, stopped in their tracks. On the golf range, Rory McIlroy — a week ahead of the 2012 British Open at Royal Lytham & St Annes — was involved in a fun challenge set up by one of his sponsors, EA Sports. To most observers on this July day, it seemed a challenge even beyond the powers of McIlroy, a player who had claimed his first career Major at the 2011 US Open. The organisers had positioned a full-sized soccer goal some 150 yards down the range; McIlroy's task was to hit the crossbar with one of the Titleist balls which were usually reserved for spinning on to manicured greens in one part of the world or another.

McIlroy embraced the challenge with a gusto that told of his competitive spirit as much as a fun-loving side that manifested itself in a grin which never left his face. Finally, after a number of near-misses, the golfer's ball clattered into the crossbar, and the sound of rubber meeting metal — confirmation of the hit — worked its way back to McIlroy who was already punching the air in delight. Those hotel guests who had stopped to look, captured the moment with their camera phones, the images highlighting how one of golf's genuine superstars took pleasure from succeeding in the novelty challenge, a diversion from the rigours of championship golf.

The past year and a bit had been a life-changer for McIlroy. He had followed his meltdown at the us Masters in April 2011 with a sensational bounce-back victory in his very next Major, the us Open at Congressional Country Club. He had also met the Danish tennis player Caroline Wozniacki, and their jet-set relationship, dubbed 'Wozilroy' and often lived in the eyes of the paparazzi, was one which involved the two international sporting icons mastering the art of time management and arranging the demands of tournament schedules and sponsors' demands with the need for finding their own space.

'A lot has changed, which is a good thing I think, because change is good and you have to develop. I suppose you have to grow into your own skin in a way and I felt I did a lot of that last year with a few changes, personally and professionally. I think they've all been for the good,' said McIlroy.

Up to that point in July, McIlroy's season had been a mixture of the great and the good along with some below-average performances. In October 2011 McIlroy changed management companies, from International Sports Management to Horizon Sports and, whether by coincidence or design, the move brought about a period where the Northern Irishman appeared invincible: he won three times worldwide in the winter–spring period, including the Honda Classic in March.

That win in the Honda Classic took McIlroy to No. 1 on the official world golf rankings and he continued to knock on the door in subsequent events, finishing third in the WGC-Cadillac Championship and runner-up in the Wells Fargo tournament at Quail Hollow.

By the time McIlroy reached Wentworth in May for the PGA European Tour's flagship event, the BMW PGA Championship, he had dipped in form, and a missed cut there on the back of a missed cut at the Players in Florida led to the player admitting that he had 'taken my eye off the ball,' adding, 'I did not practise as hard as I might.' He would set about rectifying that situation. One of the first initiatives was to take his long-time coach Michael Bannon out on tour with him full-time. It was to be a stroke of genius.

On that sponsor's day at the Grove — where his crossbar challenge was but one part of a fun day which also involved competing on PlayStation in an online game of Tiger Woods 2013 with some competition winners — McIlroy reflected on his season to that point. 'I've had this run after Quail Hollow where there's been four missed cuts but, even in that, there's been two top-10s and a big chance to win in Memphis [St Jude Classic] which I should have done. I still see the positives in it and see enough good stuff that it really gives me a bit of confidence going forward.

'It's still been a great year already, with getting to [world] No. 1 and winning Honda and that run. Even though it's been a bit of a barren spell the last few weeks, looking at the world rankings, I've still accumulated the second most points of anyone this year, just behind Tiger. So, I still feel like it's been a pretty successful first half of the year, even though the last few weeks haven't been great.'

Two of the season's four Majors had come and gone, however, with a large element of disappointment: he finished tied-40th at the Masters, a year on from his final round collapse when he had the Green Jacket in his grasp, only to lose a grip on it, and he had missed the cut in the us Open at the Olympic Club in San Francisco. In the following week's Open at Royal Lytham & St Annes, McIlroy would finish tied-60th. Another disappointment. The us PGA Championship at Kiawah Island, South Carolina, represented McIlroy's last shot at glory for 2012!

———

Since the win by Pádraig Harrington in the 2007 British Open ended a 60-year drought which went back to Fred Daly's pioneering annexing of the Claret Jug, Irish players — the baton passed by Harrington to the Northern Ireland triumvirate of Graeme McDowell, Rory McIlroy and Darren Clarke — had enjoyed unprecedented success in the Major championships that define careers and make players a part of golfing history.

McIlroy's performances in the Masters, the us Open and the British Open were disappointing, but at each of those championships in 2012, it would not have stretched the realms of possibility than an Irish player could have won at Augusta National, the Olympic Club or Royal Lytham & St Annes: Harrington finished tied-eighth in the Masters, only held back by a cold putter in the final round of that Sunday in April as Bubba Watson claimed a maiden Major; McDowell was runner-up to another first-time winner, Webb Simpson, in the us Open in June where Harrington again contended, finishing tied-fourth; and, in the British Open in July, McDowell was again at the business end of affairs, where he was in the final pairing for a second successive Major, but ultimately had to settle for fifth place behind South Africa's Ernie Els.

The strong showings by Irish players in each of the year's first three Majors only served to confirm that these championships, once viewed as the preserve of others, were fair game. Ireland, as a golfing nation, with players from both the Republic and Northern Ireland, had stepped into a new league and now continually punched above its weight, certainly as far as population was concerned. What Irish golf lacked in numbers, it made up for in sheer quality.

The 94th PGA Championship was held at Kiawah Island, a Pete Dye-designed seaside course — with no fewer than 10 holes fronting the Atlantic Ocean and all 18 holes offering sea views — on a barrier island in South Carolina. It was the first Major ever held in the southern state. The PGA of America's decision to bring the Major, known as 'Glory's Last Shot', to the course was a bold one. Nobody could argue with the quality of the course, but its location — over 20 miles from Charleston, the nearest major centre of population — was remote, with only one road in and out of the resort, and spectators forewarned that journey times would be slow and arduous. The other factor which made the decision to bring the PGA to Kiawah Island in August potentially problematic was the weather: hurricane season had started!

A Major championship had been a long time working its way to South Carolina, given the area's history with the sport. As far back as 1743, a Charleston merchant, David Deas, had received a shipment of 432 golf balls and 96 clubs from Scotland so that he and his friends could play a primitive form of golf. By 1786, a year before the US Constitution was adopted, residents of Charleston were playing the game on pastureland in the city. It is believed to be the first organised playing of the sport in the USA.

Kiawah Island was a more modern development. The striking aspect of the resort getting the go-ahead to stage the 1991 Ryder Cup was that it hadn't yet been built when the decision was made! That the course was actually constructed in time to stage one of the most notorious Ryder Cups in history — it became known as the 'War on the Shore' — was, many would say, a miracle. The 1991 Ryder Cup had originally been awarded to La Quinta, a resort in California. However, when concerns were raised about staging the event on a desert course and also its viability for television — given the eight-hour time difference between the west coast of America and Britain, where the BBC had the live broadcasting rights — a compromise was reached. Landmark, the company which signed the deal with the PGA of America, offered a solution: bring the match to Kiawah Island. It was 1989, and they had two years to build the course.

Build it they did, but not without its share of problems. The main one was Hurricane Hugo. Pete Dye, a modern legend when it came to designing courses, was selected to bring his architectural acumen to transforming swamp-land populated by alligators into a course that befitted the Ryder Cup. 'I'm like a kid with a lollipop,' Dye said at the time. 'This is the best piece of land I've worked on in the Northern Hemisphere.'

Dye's vision was to loop nine holes clockwise to the east along the stretch of oceanfront and to loop the back nine counterclockwise to the west. The first earth was moved in July 1989. Two months later, much of the early work was undone. Hurricane Hugo swept up from the Caribbean in September and ravaged the site: trees were pulled from the ground, sand dunes were pummelled. 'A wondrous mess' is how Dye described the aftermath of nature's fury. Against all the odds, Dye and his hardworking team not only got the course ready: it opened to rave reviews from players. And it played host to a Ryder Cup that went to the very last putt of the last match on the final green of the final day. The USA won, with Europe's Bernhard Langer remembered as the fall guy.

By the time the 2012 US PGA Championship was staged there, Kiawah Island had established a strong reputation as one of the finest courses in the United States. When the 1997 World Cup of Golf was staged there, Ireland's Paul McGinley and Pádraig Harrington emerged as the victors. And when the 2003 World Cup was held on the course, South Africans Trevor Immelman (who later became a Major champion when winning the 2008 US Masters) and Rory Sabbatini were the victors.

For its first staging of the PGA — the fourth and final Major of any given year — Kiawah Island had increased its length to 7,676 yards with a par of 72. When anyone suggested it would be 'a beast', very few disagreed.

———

Rory McIlroy's early-summer woes, if that's what they were, when he missed four cuts in five tournaments, showed signs of recovery in the WGC-Bridgestone Invitational at Akron, Ohio, in the week before the US PGA. Something clicked in his swing, and he finished fifth in a tournament with serious prize money, won by Keegan Bradley ahead of his defence of the Wanamaker Trophy, and McIlroy made the journey to the south with the endorphins flowing. He felt good.

On the Monday, McIlroy was pointed to his designated locker. Perfect! The locker was right by the window, overlooking the putting green, with unspoilt views to the beach — where he would spend many an afternoon during the week with fitness coach Steve McGregor working with a physio ball — and beyond that to the Atlantic Ocean. He thought to himself, 'I just have a good feeling about this week, something about this just feels right.'

When he met his caddie J. P. Fitzgerald, McIlroy repeated those thoughts in words. Fitzgerald wasn't surprised. He'd seen how well McIlroy struck the ball in Akron. In fact, heading into the British Open, Fitzgerald had told other members of the player's backroom team that something big was afoot. If not that week, down the road. 'The way this guy is hitting the ball, he is going to destroy fields,' Fitzgerald had said. Little did he realise how prophetic those words would be.

——

One of the dangers in bringing the US PGA to South Carolina in August was the possibility of inclement weather. The locals would tell you that the hurricane season had started, although the greater probability was for thunderstorms. So proved to be the case. On the Tuesday, lightning bolts gave an electric zigzagging pattern to the skies and players tried to fit in their practice schedules between cloud bursts.

Players were also digesting information, confirmed at registration, that the PGA of America had decided there would be no bunkers on the links, just 'sandy areas' where players would be allowed to 'lightly' ground their clubs should the ball finish in such waste areas or in the 'bunkers' which were no more.

In dismissing any suggestion that the rule had been brought in to avoid a repeat of the situation at Whistling Straits in 2010, when Dustin Johnson missed out on a play-off after incurring a two-stroke penalty for 'grounding' his club in a bunker which wasn't clearly defined, the PGA's Kerry Haigh said: 'We look at each course on its own merits and this is a totally different design, a unique design. It's all sand-based. Whistling Straits is not.'

The other talking point in the locker room among players concerned the grass which had been introduced on to the greens. The original Bermuda grasses used on the greens and the tee complexes had succumbed to the high levels of salt in the irrigation waters and had even led to the course's closure in the summers of 2002 and 2003. With the help of Pete Dye, a move was made to Seashore Paspalum, a grass with a greater degree of resistance. Players, many of them unfamiliar with its texture, experienced the new grass for the first time at Kiawah Island in the week of the PGA championship.

Tiger Woods, without a Major win since his US Open triumph of 2008, arrived as the only three-time winner on the PGA Tour. His three wins in a season that saw him leapfrog up the world rankings like a gazelle, had come in Arnold Palmer's tournament at Bay Hill,

Jack Nicklaus's tournament — the Memorial — at Muirfield Village, and his own tournament — the AT&T — at Congressional. A bit like McIlroy, though, Woods had disappointed in the Majors: tied-40th at the Masters, tied-21st at the US Open (having shared the midway lead) and, only at the British Open, had he contended to the death where he eventually finished tied-third.

As he prepared to claim a 15th Major win of his career in his on-going quest to eat into Nicklaus's record of 18, Woods was upbeat despite a poor record — just one win in 24 — on courses designed by Pete Dye. His victory in the 2001 Players championship at Sawgrass was the exception to the rule. Woods borrowed the belief of old pros that whatever course you're playing in any given week is your favourite course, as he contemplated his assault on the 94th US PGA.

'There's a lot of mounding and a lot of movement in his designs, a lot of it is visual. There's a lot more room out there, whether it's on the fairways or on the greens, than you think. He just makes you look the other way, and he's a masterful designer in that way . . . . he makes you think, which I like, instead of just going out there and hitting a golf ball.

'He makes you make decisions off the tee, he makes you make decisions into the greens and makes you leave a ball in the right spot. The thing about Pete is, if you miss your spots, you're going to get penalised severely,' said Woods, who had moved up to world No. 2, behind Luke Donald in the rankings, heading into the Major.

———

A quintet of Irish players were in the field for the final Major of the 2012 season. Michael Hoey, his career on an upward graph and with two titles on the PGA European Tour to his name inside a year — the Dunhill Links and the Trophée Hassan II — earned a special invite from the PGA of America. The Belfastman joined the four Major champions — Pádraig Harrington, Graeme McDowell, Rory McIlroy and Darren Clarke — in a field that included 99 of the top-100 players in the world. American Ben Crane, who pulled out prior to the championship with a back injury, was the odd man out.

The five Irish players had taken different approaches towards preparing for the PGA: Harrington's world ranking didn't get him into the field for the WGC-Bridgestone Invitational, so the Dubliner had taken in the Reno-Tahoe Open, preferring to play with a card in his hand the week before a Major; Darren Clarke had come in off a two-week family holiday in the Bahamas, whilst G-Mac, Hoey and McIlroy had all competed in Akron.

Of them all, McIlroy's preparation was the most unusual. Having checked in on the Monday, the man from Holywood limited his play of the course to nine holes that first day and the other nine holes on Tuesday. The process had partly to do with the weather, the irregular thunderstorms proving disruptive, but also to a sense that he liked the course and felt good about his game. On the eve of the championship, McIlroy — relaxed and at ease — was rather conservative in his public utterings. Asked what his aim was for the season's final Major, he replied: 'To get into contention, to give myself a chance to win on Sunday. If I feel like I have a decent chance going into Sunday, that's all I can ask for.'

In his march to a maiden Major title in the US Open at Congressional, the weather gods collaborated by offering a soft course primed for his ability to hit the ball long and straight off the tee. The conditions — aided by thunderstorms on 14 of the previous 15 days — seemed to offer an eerily familiar scenario heading into the PGA, even if one significant difference was that the wind coming in off the Atlantic brought heavier air and ensured the ball didn't travel as far as an inland parkland course.

McIlroy, though, was conscious — more than anyone — that he'd under-performed in the season's opening three Majors. 'It's a little bit of pressure, that you want to do well at the last Major of the season, but I am inspired by the way I played last week [in Akron] and, if I can bring that form into this week and hit the ball well, then I should fare better,' he said.

No player underestimated the severity of the Ocean Course. As Adam Scott, the fall guy in the previous month's British Open, confessed: 'There's no secret recipe to it . . . . you've got to start with a focus on ball-striking and take it from there. If you can hit some fairways and greens, you're going to give yourself a chance to score well.'

The first three winners of the year's Majors had extended the sequence of different winners to 16 since Pádraig Harrington's win in the US PGA of 2008. Bubba Watson was a first-time Major winner when collecting the Masters, where he beat Louis Oosthuizen in a play-off, and Webb Simpson (who would miss the British Open due to the imminent arrival of his baby daughter) followed by taking the US Open. Ernie Els, aided by Scott's collapse, rejoined the Major club when he reclaimed the Claret Jug ten years after his first win.

Of those players who hadn't won a title in the season's first three Majors, McDowell had proven the most consistent. The man known as G-Mac got into contention time and time again and actually played in the final pairing of back-to-back final round pairings: he finished 12th in the Masters, second in the US Open and fifth in the British Open.

'Yeah, a strong year in the Majors for me . . . . fingers crossed, we'll give it a good run this week,' said McDowell, who suggested the grass on the greens would be a factor for many players. 'This Paspalum grass has a little bit of grain to it. It kind of grows down the slopes, which means some of these steep banked run-off areas, you can't kind of pitch a nine-iron into the slope and hope that it's going to hop up with some pace. Really the first bounce digs in. It's very soft. I see a lot of these run-off areas. You'll see a lot of guys putting, just to try and get something rolling quick so that it doesn't dig into this grain.'

Playing into and then putting on the Paspalum grass was new to the majority of the field, but not to all: the likes of McIlroy, Luke Donald, Keegan Bradley and Dustin Johnson were well used to it, as that type of grass was also in use at the Bears Club in Florida where they were based and practised. '[We] might have an advantage because we are used to how it reacts and we practise on that stuff in our off-weeks,' said McIlroy.

———

Anyone with an early tee-time in the first round of the 94th US PGA Championship was entitled to cast their eyes upwards to the clear skies and thank their lucky stars. No scattered thunderstorms. No wind. And, as Rory McIlroy looked out across the gentle sand hills towards the ocean waters lapping up on to the shore in that Thursday morning sunshine, he went through his pre-round routine on the range and later on the putting green, aware that the course was there for the taking.

Any links course, regardless of its length, required some assistance from the weather gods in order to bare its teeth. But the much-vaunted and much-feared Ocean Course was left to its own devices as the championship got under way with barely a breath of wind. The early starters made hay whilst the sun shone, and the wind only picked up as they, the first wave of players, were well into their rounds. The second wave — in the afternoon, with two tee starts off the first and the 10th holes — had a tougher time of it, without question.

McIlroy hardly put a foot wrong. When the Northern Irishman did make an error, such as a pulled tee-shot on the par 3 17th where alligators lurked in the pond between the tee complex and the green, he got unintentional assistance from a member of the gallery. The errant ball hit her on the hip and then ricocheted back into a sandy area — a bunker to all intents and purposes — from where McIlroy splashed out to 10 feet and saved par. He then retraced his steps, and handed the ball to the uninjured woman as a souvenir.

He could allow himself a little grin at his good fortune. In the previous month's British Open at Royal Lytham & St Annes, McIlroy's tee shot on the 15th hole had struck a teenager on the head and careered off beyond the out-of-bounds stakes. This time, he had been the beneficiary. 'It's becoming a habit in the Majors, I'll try not to do that again,' remarked McIlroy. On that occasion, McIlroy had not only signed a glove for the boy, but also put him up in a local hotel after discovering he was camping out with friends in a tent.

More importantly for McIlroy, the par save on the 17th — a par 3 of 229 yards with trouble all around the green — enabled him to keep momentum en route to an opening round of 67, five-under-par, that left him positioned nicely.

McIlroy got off on the right foot with a birdie on the opening hole, the 10th, where he rolled in a 12-footer, and he went on to shoot a bogey-free round that featured a further four birdies. 'It was flat calm and I really thought I had to take advantage of the conditions. I have a great platform to go on from . . . . overall, [67] was a fair reflection of how I played,' admitted the 23-year-old Ulsterman.

As he acknowledged, work with his short game guru Dave Stockton in Akron the previous week contributed to his comfort levels. 'We made a slight adjustment to my routine and my stroke, and it made a huge difference. I felt so much better on the greens than I did at the [British] Open. He said to me, "You know, just go out there and have fun and enjoy it and smile." That's something that I've really tried to do, and it's definitely helped.'

McIlroy nibbled on just one energy bar through his round but consumed copious bottles of water. 'You have to have the right attitude going out there. You have to realise that to give yourself a chance going into the final day of a Major, there's still 54 holes to play, and especially on this golf course, middles of greens are totally okay. Every time you hit it in the middle of the green, you're going to have a chance, especially the way the greens are rolling. For me, it's just about giving myself as many chances as possible.'

He used the driver 10 times in the opening round, more often than not finding a place on the soft fairways. He didn't drop a shot all day and, although he failed to birdie two of the par 5s, he picked up a shot on the field on the par 3 14th hole, measuring all of 249 yards, where he hit a towering three-iron to 12 feet and rolled in the birdie putt.

The maturity exhibited by the 23-year-old McIlroy was matched by a 34-year-old Swede. Carl Pettersson had won the regular tour stop in South Carolina — the Heritage tournament at Hilton Head — in April and took better advantage of the conditions than anyone on the opening day. Pettersson, a naturalised American, shot an opening round 66 that gave him a one-stroke lead over McIlroy, Spain's Gonzalo Fernandez-Castano, Sweden's Alex Noren and American Gary Woodland, who had endured a troubled season caused by rupturing a cyst in his wrist when competing in the Masters tournament at Augusta.

The fearsome reputation of the Ocean Course proved to be unwarranted on that first day of play in the 94th PGA Championship. Pettersson, who had moved to the United States as a teenager, who had attended college in North Carolina, and who had taken out American citizenship in 2011, held the lead. What's more, he was a proponent of the belly putter — an endangered species as far as the R&A and the USGA were concerned — and had made a good start in maintaining a sequence of Major winners who had used such a device. Keegan Bradley in the 2011 US PGA; Webb Simpson in the 2012 US Open; Ernie Els in the 2012 British Open.

———

One sign was more evident than any other on the island. For those golfers who acquired housing, those local residents who used bicycles to make their way to the tournament, or for spectators coming in by road from Charleston and other urban areas, the warning was clear: 'DANGER ALLIGATORS'!

For good reason. Kiawah Island — and its 183 ponds — was home to one of the largest populations of the reptiles in South Carolina and, if the common advice was to run in a zigzag should an alligator decide to give chase, the law was very clearly on the side of the cold-blooded, scaly creatures. Spectators attending the championship were advised it was against the law to harass or harm alligators in any way and never to approach within 60 feet of them, with the added warning that, despite their lethargic appearance, they were actually capable of moving at great speed over short distances.

———

Oh, what a difference a day makes! Friday's second round of the PGA Championship. The beast awoke from its slumbers, and how. A stiff wind blew in off the Atlantic; the Ocean Course, a mere pussycat for the first round, was transformed as it bared its teeth and provided a severe examination for the players attempting to claim the Wanamaker Trophy, the largest of all the Major championship silverware.

From the time the first players made their way to the first and 10th tees shortly before 7.30 am, the flags atop the giant scoreboard on the 18th green and various other points around the course blew with a fierceness that tested the strength of the fabric. The scoring average was 78 — the highest in US PGA history for any round since the championship moved to a strokeplay format in 1958, when the previous record of 76.8 was set at Llanerch Country Club — and there were only four registered rounds under par: Vijay Singh (69), Tiger Woods (71), Phil Mickelson (71) and Ian Poulter (71).

Another player, Northern Ireland's Michael Hoey, had battled magnificently to a 70. However, in identifying his ball in one of the sand areas midway through his round, he had failed to replicate the original lie and brought the transgression to the attention of the PGA officials. Having already signed his card, he was disqualified.

It was a tough day on the course. No fewer than 41 players failed to break 80 on that Friday and the unfortunate club professional, Doug Wade from Ohio, had the distinction of recording the day's highest score, a 93 that mercifully left him one shy of the worst score in PGA Championship history.

The man with most to smile about was Singh, the 49-year-old Fijian who managed to record a 69 that moved him into a three-way share of the 36-holes lead on 140, four-under-par, with Woods and first-round leader Pettersson.

Singh — who had recorded top-10 finishes in his last two outings prior to the PGA, at the British Open and the Canadian Open — claimed he had put actual scoring out of his mind, in concentrating on playing one shot at a time. 'After a while you don't really think about your score. You just think about each hole, each shot and just try not to mess up. It was so hard just standing on the greens trying to make a putt,' he said, in giving an insight into dealing with the 30-miles-an-hour winds.

'It was tough out there. Wow!' said Woods, after reaching the midpoint in a share of the lead for a second Major of the season. He had got into a similar position at the US Open at the Olympic Club, only to fade away surprisingly over the weekend, a time when he traditionally got the job done in amassing his career total of 14 Majors.

Woods had used his putter as a saviour for much of his first two rounds. And, although positioned where he wanted to be atop the leaderboard at the half-way point, Woods demonstrated a touch of frailty in his play of the 501 yards par 4 18th hole where he hooked his tee-shot, only to be saved by the corporate tent down the left of the fairway. His ball bounced back into play, to a trampled down area, from where he found the green. Then, his putter deserted him. He three-putted for bogey.

As Graeme McDowell observed after his round, 'It's brutal, one of the toughest set-ups I think I've seen at a major championship in a long time. Is it unfair? I mean, this is the PGA Championship. You've got to go out there and battle it out, and someone is going to win the tournament this weekend. You've got to hang tough out there.'

Hoey's disqualification deprived the Irish quintet of a clean sweep in making the cut. The four Irish Major champions in the field, however, all survived: McIlroy added a 75 to his opening 67; McDowell shot a 76 to go with his first round 68; Harrington also had a 76 to add to his first day's 70; and Clarke followed up his 73 with a 76.

The course played so difficult in the second round that afternoon tee times were delayed as the early wave of players sought to combat the conditions. 'The golf shots this golf course asks you to hit time and time and time again, you really have to hit phenomenal golf shots. The room for error is tiny,' said Ian Poulter.

One of those phenomenal shots was hit by Rory McIlroy on the par 3 14th, a hole of 238 yards that played to an average of 3.45 in the second round. McIlroy hit a four-iron — perfectly executed, one of the shots he'd worked on with coach Michael Bannon during the year — and held the green. What's more, he rolled home the birdie putt for one of only five birdies recorded there all day. 'I limited the damage as much as I could and I'm in a good position going into the weekend. I can't really ask for more,' said McIlroy.

———

Moving day. The weather forecasters predicted — rightly — that a storm front would move in over the Ocean Course during the afternoon of Saturday's third round. But there was no early start to outwit the storms, no change to the tee-times which, in reality, are aligned to facilitate primetime TV viewing. Rory McIlroy, however, had no complaints. Although his work was only half-complete when the storms arrived and forced play to be suspended, with 26 players on the course, the Northern Irishman had served notice of his intent to become a multiple Major champion.

When the horn sounded to suspend play in the afternoon, McIlroy had moved into a share of the lead — on six-under-par — with Vijay Singh. He had thrown down the gauntlet.

This was a day when the game seemed easy to McIlroy, a grind for Woods. Ironically, McIlroy's magnificence was demonstrated not by one of the five birdies he conjured up in his opening eight holes but, rather, by a par save on the par 4 third hole.

McIlroy's three-wood tee-shot was hit as straight as an arrow towards a decaying oak tree which guarded the entrance to the green. On the player's arrival to the tree, there was no sight of the ball. The more McIlroy and caddie J. P. Fitzgerald searched, the more puzzled they became. With the clock on the five-minute search period ticking down, a TV cameraman provided the answer to the conundrum: the ball had lodged between the branch and the bark of the tree.

One of the iconic images of the 94th PGA Championship was of McIlroy reaching up into the tree branches to retrieve the ball. 'I got up there and I knew the line of the ball was right on the tree. I was just like, "Well, if it hit the tree, I'm sure it's just somewhere around here in these long grass things or in the wood chip or whatever." We'd been looking for it for maybe about three minutes and then one of the guys that was working for the TV came over and said, "You know, it's actually stuck in the tree."

'I'm like, "How can it be stuck in this thing? There's no branches, no leaves for it to be stuck in." But it had wedged itself in between the tree bark and the actual tree, so I was just happy to get it up-and-down for four and move on to the next. I thought it was very important to do that,' recalled McIlroy.

The importance of the par save was that it kept McIlroy's momentum going. He'd birdied the first and second holes and went on to record further birdies at the fifth, seventh and eighth holes. His only blemish came on the par 4 ninth. But even that bogey — which came just before play was suspended — couldn't wipe the smile from his face. 'I've come here with a bit of confidence from the way I played last week [in Akron] and it's been nice to take that into this week and show it out on the golf course. There's still a lot of guys with a chance to win, still a long way to go.'

Tiger Woods was probably more pleased to hear the siren halting play than anyone else. Woods was three-over on his round through seven holes and had dropped down to tied-11th on one-under when rescued from a dreadful day on the links.

Moving day had turned out to be little more than a half-day for those at the business end of the championship. McIlroy, though, wasn't complaining. He was positioned exactly where he wanted to be. 'I'm going into the final day of the final Major of the season tied for the lead, so I can't ask for much more. I don't care if it's going to be 27 holes, 18 holes, 36 holes. I'm just happy to be going in there in a good position.'

———

Rory McIlroy's alarm clock sounded shortly after 5 am on Sunday morning. It signalled another day of destiny, as he made his way from the rented house on Kiawah Island which he shared with his father Gerry and his management team to the Ocean Course.

Players started to gather on the range from 6.15 am, with Woods — seeking to rescue his poor play of Saturday — among the early arrivals. The magic, though, had gone in his case. Sunday proved to be as frustrating as his Saturday, and Woods became a bit player in the drama that unfolded.

Indeed, McIlroy ensured that Sunday became a one-man show. By the time he finished his third round, the man who fashioned his game as a youngster at Holywood Golf Club, outside Belfast, had opened up a three-stroke lead over Carl Pettersson. He signed for a third round 67 and, aware that destiny was in his own hands, headed back to the house to catch up on his sleep. It was a measure of McIlroy's comfort zone that the sleep wasn't of the cat-nap variety. He actually fell into a deep sleep, with the result that his dad had to wake him up with a reminder that there was unfinished business at hand.

McIlroy only got to the course half an hour before his scheduled tee-time, where he was grouped with Pettersson — now his chief pursuer — and American Bo Van Pelt. It was plenty of time. He timed his arrival to the first tee for the final round to perfection, with seven minutes to spare. The period before his next step towards fulfilling his destiny was spent pitching on the short game area behind the bleachers: 11 chips to various flag positions, another five from the sandy waste area. A total of 16 shots, and then that jaunty walk to the tee.

For much of the preceding tee-times, the Wanamaker Trophy had been positioned on a perch to the right of the tee. Shortly before McIlroy made his way from the short game area to the tee, where Pettersson was handed McIlroy's card to mark, the trophy was moved to the left-hand side so that the players in the final three-ball walked directly by it. They were left in no doubt what they were playing for, a trophy engraved with the legends of the sport.

Prior to his final round, someone had asked McIlroy if he was concerned about the number of players — Adam Scott at the

British Open at Royal Lytham & St Annes, Jim Furyk in the previous week's wgc-Bridgestone Invitational — who had lost final-round leads. It seemed an odd question, certainly untimely. But McIlroy took it in his stride. 'A lot of guys that haven't held on in the past, it's been a first-time experience for them. I learned a lot from the Masters last year, that's something I can think back to and draw on . . . . at least being in that position before, I'll know what to do again. Augusta will stand me in good stead.'

With the sun shining and hardly any wind, the final three-ball had barely got their respective quests for glory under way than Pettersson was subjected to a ruling that impacted on the dynamics of the final round.

Pettersson's planned assault was scuppered from the start after he fell victim to a rules infringement. In playing his ball from a lateral water hazard on the first hole, his club touched a loose leaf on the back swing. He was assessed a two-stroke penalty for a breach of Rule 13-4c. Before making the stroke, he asked the rules official if he was allowed to touch grass, in the hazard, with his club, prior to the stroke. Pettersson was correctly informed that he could do so, provided that he did not ground the club in the hazard.

In making his backswing, Pettersson's club brushed the grass behind the ball (not a breach) and at the same time moved a leaf (loose impediment), in breach of the rule. His par on the hole became a double-bogey, and the Swede was only informed of the additional shots after he teed off from the fourth hole. To his credit, Pettersson responded by running off three birdies in a row from the fourth but always had too much daylight between himself and McIlroy.

Instead, for much of the round, McIlroy's chief pursuer turned out to be Ian Poulter who reeled off five straight birdies to launch his quest for a breakthrough Major title. Poulter took just 31 strokes on his front nine, only for his challenge to disintegrate on the homeward run when he ran up four bogeys in his closing six holes. He eventually finished with a 69 for 284 that had promised so much more, but ultimately left him in a share of third.

As it transpired, another Englishman, David Lynn — only playing on an invite from the PGA of America — closed with a 68 for 283, five-under, that enabled him to finish alone in second place.

McIlroy could do no wrong, his performance every bit as imperious as the one that had enabled him to capture his breakthrough Major win in the US Open at Congressional. He secured his second career Major with a bogey-free final round 66 for 275, 12-under-par. It gave him a record eight strokes winning margin over Lynn. When he rolled in a birdie putt on the 18th to put the icing on the cake, the roars from those gathered around the finishing hole reached a crescendo. McIlroy — wearing a red Oakley shirt, similar in colour to ones worn by Tiger Woods in the final round of the Majors — raised his arms to the heavens.

Fitzgerald joined him in the salute. So did the crowds.

As McIlroy, a multiple Major champion, left the green, his father embraced him. The tears welled up in the golfer's eyes. 'Stop crying,' quipped the dad, the man who had introduced his son to the sport as a two-year old.

———

Rory McIlroy's post-round duties involved a seemingly endless number of photo calls — on the 18th green, on the beach, in the media centre — and, through it all, the Boy Wonder took it all in his stride. Just as he had done on the golf course, where his deeds were acknowledged by his peers.

As Graeme McDowell, the winner of the 2010 US Open put it, 'He's going to be the player that kids look up to, that kids measure their wannabe games by. Ten years ago, it was Tiger Woods. It is still Tiger Woods to a certain extent but, now, we've got superstars like Rory McIlroy for kids to be looking at with the double-hit snap or whatever the hell he calls it.

'I mean, [he's] got great attitude with great charisma and great character. That's pretty much it in a nutshell. He's great for the game, an absolute breath of fresh air for the game of golf.'

Of being a role model, McIlroy was honest. 'I realise that every time my face is on TV or I'm playing in a tournament, that I am a role model for a lot of people and a lot of kids do look up to me. I try to do my best in that regard and put myself across as honestly and as modestly as possible. Some can view it as a big responsibility, but I think if you just go about your life and live it normally and live it the way you always would, I think everything's okay. But you know, it's a huge honour to be put in that position to have an effect on so many people's lives, it's a nice feeling.'

McIlroy's celebrations on the Sunday night of his second Major win involved watching re-runs on the 'Golf Channel' and a couple of Diet Cokes. An early alarm call, 27 holes — with eight birdies and just one bogey — and, at the end of it, the Wanamaker Trophy. He was tired.

The next day, he was up early — and back at the course — for photo shoots for Oakley, followed by a plane trip to Cincinnati where he joined girlfriend Caroline Wozniacki.

His other life.

Away from golf.

Postscript ∽

IN SEARCH OF AN ELUSIVE GREEN JACKET . . .

On the eve of the 2009 US Masters at Augusta National Golf Club, Lee Westwood approached Pádraig Harrington. 'What's all this about the Paddy Slam? Are you taking up wrestling?' quipped the Englishman to the Irishman.

All joking aside, Harrington went into that first Major of the year in an exulted position. As the winner of the 2008 British Open at Royal Birkdale and the US PGA championship at Oakland Hills in Detroit, the Dubliner was set the task of extending his Major-winning streak to three. In the modern era, only Tiger Woods — who won the US Open, the British Open and the US PGA in 2000, and went on to add the US Masters in 2001 — had performed such a feat.

Of his chances of adding the Masters to his CV, Harrington at the time was bullish. 'It's a Major. It's a chance to win another Major. It's a chance to win the Masters. All of those things bring their own pressure. Just because it's three in a row adds to it, but not significantly . . . I'm going to have that pressure for the foreseeable future in Majors. I'm going to turn up to a lot of them and know that if I play my game, I can win.'

As it transpired, that 2009 Masters turned out to be a step too far for Harrington. The third leg of what had been dubbed the 'Paddy Slam' came to a halt. But not for the want of trying. For the truth of the matter is that, for as long as he is in the field for the Masters, Harrington will try his ultimate to win. It is the only way he knows.

On Sunday 8 April 2012, Bubba Watson made the walk from the Butler Cabin to the practice putting green at Augusta National, where a helicopter hovered overhead as South African Charl Schwartzel placed the Green Jacket — traditionally presented to the winner of the Masters by the previous year's champion — on to Watson's slight shoulders.

At one point Watson thought of asking Schwartzel — a qualified pilot — what type of helicopter was in the skies above the pine trees. But he thought better of it. The jacket was more important.

That walk from the immaculately white-front cabin to the green takes no more than two minutes and usually entails the champion — with green-coated club members and a Pinkerton security escort — making his way through a guard of honour of patrons who have stayed much longer than the winning to ensure that the year's newest winner is given a fitting accolade.

It is the only box left for an Irish golfer to tick in terms of winning a Major.

Who would ever have thought that Harrington's win in the 2007 British Open at Carnoustie would have opened the flood-gates in the manner that followed? Or how he would go on to successfully defend the Claret Jug at Royal Birkdale? Or how he would lift the 27 lb Wanamaker trophy as the US PGA champion at Oakland Hills?

Or how a succession of Northern Irishmen would follow in his footsteps as Major champions: Graeme McDowell in the us Open at Pebble Beach in 2010; Rory McIlroy in the us Open at Congressional Country Club in 2011; and Darren Clarke in the Open at Royal St George's in 2011. Then, McIlroy, again, in claiming a second career Major in the 2012 us PGA Championship at Kiawah Island.

One box left to tick for an Irish Slam: the Masters!

On the same evening that Watson's wizardry had seen him execute a shot from the pine straw — from under the hanging limbs of cathedral pines and other fauna — to defeat South Africa's Louis Oosthuizen at the second hole of a sudden death play-off to win his first Masters, the Irish Major champions exited down Magnolia Lane with renewed belief that one day the grand prize could be theirs.

Harrington had been in contention for much of the final round, only for a putter that seemed to have been placed in a bucket of ice overnight to stay stubbornly cold. In the end he settled for eighth place and drove out on to Washington Road and its mass of strip malls and fast food joints in the knowledge that there would be years ahead for other chances. 'I would love to win a Masters. The Masters is a tremendous examination. It's a tough track, it really is. Your distance control has to be really good and you have to putt and chip and drive it really well. But there's nothing I can do about it . . . It's not like I can turn up and wave a magic wand to say that I am going to win. I can only just play my game and do my thing and if it happens, it happens.'

Harrington — who chopped and changed some of his back-up team in 2011 in the ongoing quest to claim more Major titles — has remained philosophical through the good and the occasional bad times. As he has put it: 'I've got some experience over 20 years (in golf) of the highs and the lows of sport, and that's the one thing that will stand by me. What brings me tremendous confidence is that I have not always won as a rule. Winning is a habit and some people have that habit and no understanding of losing.

'I have plenty of understanding of losing and I've had to work my way through some pretty miserable (times) in terms of golf. I'd a record of second places (at one point) and it was being used as a stick to beat me with. But you work through that and it gives you tremendous experience. To be honest, you learn from losing. You don't really learn from winning, even though winning is a habit.'

If McDowell — who made only his second cut in five attempts at the Masters — didn't quite leave with Harrington's jauntiness, the Ulsterman's trip home to his house in Lake Nona, Florida, was also made with a sense that he had finally worked out a way to play the Augusta National course and that the future would be far less intimidating.

In both 2010 and 2011, McDowell had left downhearted and downbeat. The course had mauled him, and he had missed the cut on each occasion. His 2012 Masters — despite having opened with a 75 — was an encouraging one. 'I'd love to win a Green Jacket, so I've got to come back here every year and I've got to learn to hit around this golf course . . . You can do all the preparation you like, and then the tournament starts and you hit it in the wrong place and you've got to get yourself out of that position. Any under-par rounds under your belt (around Augusta) are nice and good for the experience going forward.'

———

Rory McIlroy had gone into the 2012 Masters as one of the pre-championship favourites and had been well positioned to challenge for a second Major to add to his 2011 US Open. It wasn't to be, as his poor third round — when he was paired with Spain's Sergio García — saw him fall down the leaderboard.

The previous year, it had been all so different: McIlroy carried a four-stroke lead into the final round, only to see the grand prize taken from his grasp as the golfing gods slung arrow after arrow in his direction.

On the morning after his meltdown, before he undertook the long journey to Malaysia where he shared a flight with Charl Schwartzel, the victor, McIlroy had cried his eyes out whilst on the phone home to his mother Rosie. 'It was the first time I had cried in a long time about anything. I sort of let it all out that morning, and I definitely felt the better of it,' he recalled a year on.

There was one other phone call of consequence after his meltdown. It came from none other than Greg Norman. In the 1996 Masters, the Great White Shark had carried a six-shot lead into the final round, only to lose by five to Nick Faldo. McIlroy was in his hotel room in Malaysia when he took the call. What had Norman told him? 'It was great coming from him, because I'm sure he knew how I felt. He said a couple of things to me that I found very useful, that I could put into practice — especially in weeks where there's so much hype and build-up, to create this little bubble around yourself and don't let any of the outside interference come in.'

Of course, by the time McIlroy returned to the Masters in 2012, his status had heightened. He'd won the US Open in record-breaking fashion and had spent time as the No. 1 player in the official world rankings. He was, as his friend McDowell had put it, the next big thing in golf, the game's newest superstar.

And each time he drives through the gates of Magnolia Lane in the first week of April for the Masters tournament, McIlroy will know that his game is tailor-made for Augusta National. It is only a matter of time before the Green Jacket is his. As Tiger Woods put it: 'You know, he has all the makings of being a great champion for a long period of time.'

Sir Nick Faldo, a six-time Major champion and the greatest European player of modern times, never managed to achieve a career Grand Slam of all four Majors. But the Englishman couldn't rule out the possibility that McIlroy, whom he first met as a teenager when competing in the Faldo Series, would one day become the first European player to achieve such a feat.

'Rory's got half of them already and he's right there, anything can happen. You can't predict anything but he now knows — and more importantly, the rest of the field knows — that when he is on they might be playing for second place,' said Faldo, after McIlroy's win in the US PGA Championship at Kiawah Island. 'Jack, Seve, Tiger, Rory are the only players to win multiple Majors under 25 [years of age], that puts you in a special line, doesn't it?'

Faldo added: 'The most important thing is to play one Major are a time. Rory now knows the most important thing in his life are the Majors and he should do everything to gear his schedule and the rest of his career for the Majors, and take one at a time.'

INDEX